Listen to what these successful business leaders have to say about the Maui Mastermind series of books for business owners!

"This book will change your life. So many business owners are pedaling as fast as they can, and not really steering. In these pages is a powerful plan with actionable steps you can and should take to build a solid foundation beneath you, and then springboard from that foundation to large scale growth and profitability. This book is the no-nonsense secret formula brought to you by business owners who truly walk the walk on the path to success."

> —Jeff Hoffman, Serial Entrepreneur
> (Priceline.com, uBid.com,
> ColorJar LLC)

"Brilliant! David and Diane will help you to not just make money building your business, but more importantly, you'll learn to do it in a way that creates true freedom. Read this book!"

> —Joseph Guerriero, Publisher,
> *Success Magazine*

"As a CPA to privately held businesses, I can't think of a more relevant book to pass along to my clients. If you want to escape the self-employment trap and build a scalable and profitable business, then this book is your road map. Apply the principles in this book and you will free-up your time, increase your business cash-flow, take home more money, ltiply the value of your business. Guarant   )f

D1042505

"As a small business owner with annual sales of $70 million, this is the book I wished I would have read 10 years ago! You better believe I'm applying what I read to my business."

> —Kiran Asher, Business Owner

Build a Business, Not a Job!

How to Build Your Business to Sell, Scale, or Own Passively

David Finkel
and Stephanie Harkness

CONTENTS

v

FOREWORD

I came to the world of business in the most unexpected way—through public education.

I was a home economics teacher in San Jose, California. I spent 13 years in public education, leaving it to start my first business, Expressions in Fine Jewelry. A gemologist friend and I created a high-end jewelry company serving personal clients. For six years, I flew around the world meeting our clients, sometimes carrying as much as $3 million worth of jewels in my briefcase. Exciting as that may seem, it got old after a while. The business needed me to be there at every step, every day, day after day. So when my husband Jack took early retirement from General Electric where he worked as an engineering manager, we made a decision that totally changed our lives. We decided to build a business together.

We looked around at various opportunities—from doing our own start-up, to buying a franchise, to purchasing an existing business. In the end, we opted to buy a small injection molding plastics manufacturing company near our home called Pacific Plastics and Engineering.

I look back and think *what in the world were we doing?!* We didn't know anything about injection molded plastic manufacturing; we had never co-owned a manufacturing business before. In my heart, I still felt like a school teacher, for heaven's sake! But both Jack and I had a deep belief in each other, and we knew we didn't want to live our lives wondering *what if. . . .* You've met those people, right? They spend the long days of their later years wondering and sighing *if only . . .* and *I wish we would have . . . .*

Well we didn't want that to be us so we stepped out into the unknown and invested $60,000—my entire retirement savings through my teacher's pension—to buy this company and go after our dreams.

I wish I could tell you it was all roses and champagne from there on, but it wasn't. Our first few months in business, we learned that all those customers the seller had told us about were less than real. And the financial books he showed us were more fiction than fact. Faced with these challenges, we did what most self-employed people do—we rolled up our sleeves and got to work. Jack took over the operations and began the painstaking process of mastering manufacturing injection molding plastics products. And I stepped into the role of running everything else—sales, marketing, financial management—as well as providing big-picture leadership of the business.

It took us three years of hard work, but we turned the business around. At that point, we needed to make a decision. Did we want it to continue as a mom-and-pop business that revolved around Jack and me, or did we want to step up and build a business that was bigger and more substantive than just the two of us? We decided to grow and scale the business.

Back then we didn't have the road map you have in this book. We didn't know how to build our core business infrastructure and systems. No one showed us the distinction of building not for control, but to establish intelligent business controls to empower the business, not just Jack and me as owners.

Still, over the following three years we managed to figure those things out and turn Pacific Plastics and Engineering into a highly successful, high-end manufacturer that runs 24/7 in the United States and has operations in China. We're celebrating our 21st year of highly profitable operations and an identity as the go-to source to launch new projects in the medical device and bio-tech world.

When in 2000 I was asked to become a board member of the National Association of Manufacturers—then chair that board for two years—I led a veritable who's who of Fortune 500 companies such as IBM and Harley Davidson. While I was intimidated at first, I took action in spite of my fears and accepted the prestigious position.

Why am I sharing all this with you? Because if I can do it, so can you. Just imagine: I was an ex-school teacher with no formal training in business who, 21 years prior, had stepped out in faith with my husband and bought a small manufacturing business. Now here I was, chairing the board of one of the largest industry associations in the country, with board members who literally led billion-dollar businesses.

I discovered that while those billion-dollar businesses boasted a few more zeros in their financials than our business did, all of us were dealing with the same challenges and the same core aspects of building a thriving business. What's more, I finally realized that anyone could successfully build a business if they just solved the known challenges that every business faces. That's exactly what Jack and I did as we built a multimillion-dollar business that was truly independent of the two of us. Sure, we loved playing in the business, but we built a core leadership team that ran the business day in, day out. It was systems reliant, with strong processes and procedures that allowed it to consistently produce exceptional value for our customers and other stakeholders. And it had a clear mission and culture that guide its operations to this day, even when we're out of the country on extended vacations.

I first met David as a client of Maui Mastermind®, when in 2004 Jack and I attended the *Maui Mastermind Wealth Summit*. At $30,000 per couple, the *Wealth Summit* may be the most exclusive business owner retreat around. Over the next few years, I enjoyed participating in the event, gaining great insights and connecting with a wonderful peer group of ambitious yet caring business owners. When I was invited to become a Maui Advisor in 2007, I was honored. I had gained so much from the community that I loved sharing my experiences with other business owners who were working to grow their businesses and design the lives they wanted.

Which brings me to this book. You're going to love it, by the way. It's like finding the secret treasure map that every business owner dreams of but rarely finds. In it you'll discover a clear, concrete road map that will take you through the entire lifecycle of your business from launch to exit. What's more, it dispels the prevailing myths and misconceptions that cause so many business owners to fail.

This is the book I wish someone would have handed me 21 years ago when I started out in my own business. Not only would it have saved me from painful, costly mistakes, but it would have relieved so much of the doubt and uncertainty I felt because of all the conflicting advice I'd received over the years.

After being involved with a number of successful start-ups in Silicon Valley, including the growth of our manufacturing business, I can tell you from my perspective as a serial entrepreneur that this road map and these distinctions are incredibly powerful. They work.

But it's up to you to put these ideas into practice—to invest the time and focused attention to follow this map and apply the concrete strategies to your business.

What's the payoff for all that effort? A multimillion-dollar business in five years or less. A reliable stream of passive income. And most important—the freedom to enjoy it.

Welcome to the Maui Mastermind community of business owners and enjoy the journey!

Stephanie Harkness
Santa Cruz, California

Welcome to what might be the most important business owners' book you'll ever read. That's a strong statement, but when you've finished reading it, you can judge for yourself.

Much of what you'll learn here is unconventional. We warn you about that up front and make no apologies for it. If conventional thinking provided the answers, all business owners would be enjoying the freedom, cash flow, and lifestyle they dream of enjoying.

What we share with you took us decades to develop and many painful mistakes to finally "get it." Our goal is to cut your learning curve by 90 percent so you can take your business straight to the next level in a tenth of the time it would have ordinarily taken.

David's Story

In 2003, I was part of a mastermind group of four highly successful business owners. Twice a year we would get together in person for a full day to brainstorm ideas to scale each other's businesses, give direct feedback on new ideas, and hold each other accountable. In fewer than 24 months, these private mastermind sessions helped me grow my business by over 400 percent!

Not only did the other group members and I own and run multiple multimillion-dollar businesses, but we were each best-selling authors

(continued)

David's Story (continued)

with overly-full speaking schedules each year. During one of these mastermind sessions, we commiserated about how so few of the attendees at the average 90-minute training class we taught actually took action on what they were learning. Sure, we might have had 500 or more people in attendance, but only a small fraction of them ended up applying what they'd been taught.

So we asked this powerful question: "What if we were designing the perfect business workshop, what would it be like? How could we flip the numbers so 95 percent of the attendees immediately applied the ideas they were learning to make a dramatic difference in their business and financial lives?"

Our list of answers included: "It would need to be over an extended period of time, not just one day." And "It would need to be in a beautiful location at a five-star resort." And most important, "We would have to pre-qualify every person who attended to make sure each was absolutely committed to playing full out and using the ideas they were learning."

At first, we were just talking hypothetically, but the ideas we were creating sounded so good I turned to my mastermind partners and said, "If you're going to be a bear, be a grizzly bear, so pull out your calendars and let's schedule this event right now." My mastermind partners looked at me like I was crazy. But they stepped up to the challenge, and that was how the very first Maui Mastermind Wealth Summit came to be.

That first year the event was sold out. Midway through the event the response was so powerful and the feedback from participants so positive, we decided to make it an annual event. It's been over eight years now, and this $30,000 week-long business owner and wealth retreat continues to be the most exclusive experience of its kind. Considering that over 60 percent of the graduates sign up to come back year after year after year, we must be doing something right!

That event became the foundation of the Maui community of business owners, with these super-successful entrepreneurs and the Maui Advisors "paying it forward" to the next generation of business owners by sharing what had made a difference in their businesses and lives. Over the past 20 years, the Maui Advisors—who teach at the various Maui Mastermind online and in-person trainings—have personally started, scaled, and sold more than $2 billion of businesses.

(continued)

David's Story (continued)

And we do our best to remain true to the Maui vision that wealth is more than just the money; it's about the quality of our relationships and impact we have on the lives of others. In addition, over the past eight years, the Maui community of business owners has raised over $5.1 million for dozens of charities around the world.

We're thrilled you've taken that all-important first step of engaging with the community by picking up this book. We believe you'll discover the insights, strategies, and road map you need to take your business to the next level.

The 7 Bottom Lines You'll Gain from This Book

In our world, time has become the real currency, so we want to lay out for you the seven bottom lines you'll get by investing your time and attention in reading this book.

Bottom Line 1. A clear understanding of how to build a business, not a job. In Chapter 1, you'll learn the greatest challenge that every entrepreneur faces and the powerful perspective shift necessary to build your dream business. You'll also learn the truth behind the four most costly business owner myths.

Bottom Line 2. Why the traditional model for building a business leads to the Self Employment Trap™ (and how you can safely side-step it!). In Chapter 2, you'll learn why building your business for control is a trap and how instead you need to build your business to one day be independent of you, the owner. You'll also learn 35 intelligent business controls you'll need to design into your company and the four building blocks of all successful businesses.

Bottom Line 3. A detailed road map through the entire lifecycle of your business from launch to exit. In Chapter 3, you'll learn the concrete action steps you need to take at each Stage and Level to build a business you can sell, scale, or own passively.

Bottom Line 4. The five functional pillars of every business (and how you can create the secure foundation upon which to scale your

business). In Chapter 4, you'll learn how to systematize your sales and marketing and grow your sales; how to build out your operational systems and organize them; how to make the right hiring decisions; how to manage your cash flow; and how to lead your business enterprise.

Bottom Line 5. Six time mastery strategies to free up a full day each week to build your business. In Chapter 5, you'll learn that it doesn't take longer hours or working nights and weekends to build your dream business. Instead, you'll learn how to upgrade your use of time so you create more value for your business in fewer working hours.

Bottom Line 6. The three biggest obstacles you face as you grow your business to the next level. In Chapter 6, you'll focus on getting real about what gets in your way to reach Level Three—and what you can do about it!

Bottom Line 7. A clear, 5-step action plan. In Chapter 7, you'll discover a powerful action plan that synthesizes all the elements you've learned and gets you into directed action.

Before we begin, however, please answer this simple but crucial question: *Are you ready to take your business to the next level?*

Crazy as it may seem, most business owners aren't ready to increase their businesses by the magnitudes we're referring to here. Sure, they can be comfortable with growing their business by 5, 10, or 15 percent a year—but doubling their business? Tripling their business? Growing it by tenfold? By one hundredfold? That's just too much for them. So they shake their heads, make their excuses, and settle for less. Less than they want, less than they dream about, less than they're capable of.

Indeed, they're so busy making excuses about why they *can't*, they don't put time and energy into focusing on how they *can*. They rationalize, invent stories, and create limiting beliefs that keep them comfortable. And all their logical excuses make sense—until you look closely at the cost of holding those limiting beliefs.

Let's start by assuming you are ready to exponentially expand your business, and you *are* willing to make the decisions and answer the tough questions that will help you do it.

The pages of this book will be quiet confirmation of what you, in your heart of hearts, know to be true about building a business. It will make such obvious sense to you that you'll wonder why every other business owner on the planet doesn't understand it. But that's the subject of a far longer book, and one we'll leave to someone else to write.

FREE Business Owner Fast Track Program! ($2,275 Value)

We've designed a powerful online training program to help you turn the ideas in this book into tangible results. Best of all, we've made this training course, called the Business Owner Fast Track Program, available to readers like you for FREE! This is our way of rewarding you for taking action and applying the ideas you'll learn in this book. For full details, including your private Access Code, see Appendix A or go to **www.MauiMastermindBook.com**.

How Will You Play Today?

We have a belief that the way we do *anything* says a whole lot about the way we do *everything*, that you play like you practice. So how will you play today? How will you approach this book? Will you step up and do the exercises we lay out for you? Will you apply the road map we share? Or will you say it's just too hard . . . that you're too busy. . . .

In life, you either get your excuses or you get your dreams, but you don't get both. Which will it be for you? Decide now. If you're not going to follow the road map we lay out for you, then we urge you to give this book to someone else and settle back into your business as it currently is. Why? Because you'll only find the strategies and distinctions you'll read about too intimidating and uncomfortable.

But if you're ready to step up and learn a better way to build your business so you have both the money and the freedom to enjoy it, then turn the page and let's get to work!

Build a Business, Not a Job

How many hours a week, on average, do you work for your business? If you're like many of the business owners we've observed, you're working 50 to 70 hours a week or *more*. When you factor in the emails handled from home at odd hours and the calls taken on nights or weekends—not to mention the time spent thinking and worrying about the business when you're away from it—the total hours you work may be much higher.

Are you still enjoying the business you're building, or has it somehow turned into more of a job? A common misconception is that business owners can take time off whenever they want. But answer these questions: How many weeks of vacation a year have you averaged over the past five years? And what did you find when you returned to the business after your time away? Was it operating smoothly, with new customers brought in and key deadlines met? Or did you find decisions stalled, projects drifting off course, and fires that needed to be put out?

Ironically, while most business owners start with the intention to assert control over their business lives, most find the concept of control is a trap. That translates into paying the ultimate price for having all the control: freedom. In fact, most business owners don't build a business; they build a job. And while the job they build for themselves gives them a sense of control over their immediate business environment, it exacts the hefty price of losing the deeper sense of control and real freedom they'd enjoy *if only they had built a business, not a job*.

Going Beyond Creating a Job

When building a business that goes beyond making a job for yourself, think of it in terms of three levels that encompass the entire lifecycle of a company from launch to exit. To get from the first level to the third level requires a road map, what the Maui Mastermind community calls the Level Three Road Map™.

The following sidebar shows an overview of this three-level model for growing your business. In later chapters, we'll progressively dive deeper into specific steps and refinements for navigating this road map to reach your destination—owning a Level Three business.

The Three Levels of Building a Business
(AKA: The Level Three Road Map)

Level One: No Control, No Freedom

You've just launched a business.

At this point, not only do you have no freedom because you're working long hours to get things going, but you have no control. You're creating your business plan, gathering your start-up capital, and launching your new venture. Typical Level One business owners are filled with a mixture of doubts and dreams, fears and ambitions. They work long hours scrambling to turn their business idea into a tangible, practical, cash-flowing enterprise.

Level Two: Control, But No Freedom

You're a full-time business owner whose business is working—as long as you do.

Now you have control, but with that control comes long hours and the sense that all the decisions, all the risks, all the responsibility—all of it—rests on your shoulders. Every day, you have to keep going because if you stop, it all ends. You have the control, but no real freedom.

Level Three: Total Control, Total Freedom

You're the owner of a business that runs without needing your presence and efforts every day.

You've got the team and systems in place so your business's success is independent of you. Working for your business is now a *choice*, not an obligation or a requirement.

The focus of the Level Three Road Map is to build a business that will ultimately be independent of you, the business owner. You start with this end—a Level Three business—clearly in mind, never wavering from your commitment to build a business that profitably delivers massive value to the market in a highly scalable fashion.

As you'll see as you progress through this book, knowing where you're heading critically changes how you build your business.

Put Your Profits on Autopilot

No doubt you've flown in an airplane before. New aviation technology is amazing. As a plane takes off, a highly trained pilot guides the plane into the air and onto its course, and then turns on the autopilot system. This system maintains the course and manages long stretches of the flight with the pilot keeping an eye on the instrument panel to troubleshoot any problems that might emerge. When the plane approaches its destination, the pilot again takes over and lands the plane.

Contrast this to a pilot flying an old-fashioned plane without autopilot. Can you imagine the strain of flying cross-country in this type of plane? Sure, it might be exciting the first time, but what if you had to keep flying each day, week after week, month after month, year after year, handling every detail of every flight?

Most business owners build businesses with no autopilot and get stuck for years sitting in the cockpit, straining to maintain the proper control, altitude, and business heading. While many of these business owners make a ton of money, the strain and lifestyle costs are great. We've all seen entrepreneurs who make $1 million or more each year, but they live, breathe, and die by their businesses. They can't get away from their businesses for more than a long weekend here and there. That doesn't feel like success and wealth. Real wealth—what we call Maui Wealth—is when you have money *and* freedom, money *and* quality of life.

The Greatest Challenge Entrepreneurs Face

For the past decade, we've worked with hundreds of thousands of entrepreneurs and business owners, helping them grow their businesses, upgrade their peer groups, and improve their lifestyles. Time after time, we're approached by intelligent, hard-working people who've become owned by the very businesses they once thought *they* owned.

The greatest challenge you'll ever face as an entrepreneur is how to build a business that's independent of you, the business owner.* As the sidebar on page 2 indicated, we call this flourishing, independent business a Level Three business.

If you've struggled with this challenge, we have a solution. We'll show you how to build a business that works *for you*, not one you have to work for—a business you can one day sell, scale, or just own passively.

We own multiple businesses that continue to operate successfully to this day with minimal input on our parts. Along with the other Maui Advisors, we've collectively started, scaled, and sold more than $2 billion of businesses. During the past 15 years, we've assisted more than 100,000 business owners in making their businesses more successful. We've helped them grow their sales, increase their cash flow, and reduce their businesses' reliance on their own work and presence every day.

The Level Three Road Map works; we've proven it. Best of all, we can show *you* how to do it.

Case Study: Tom

Three years ago, an introverted ex-engineer turned successful entrepreneur attended one of our workshops. Like many business owners who find their way to one of our live events, Tom was burned out. He owned and ran a highly successful wholesale business, but he built his company to revolve around himself, which meant long hours, high stress, and sacrifices at home. In fact, it was Tom's wife who enrolled him in the workshop and even bought him the airline ticket to attend! Tom felt he couldn't afford several days out of the office, but he listened to his wife and went anyway.

What happened when he took the concepts and strategies from the workshop home and applied them in his business? Here's what he said: *"I've always been one of those driven people who believed in working hard to reach their goals. Before I began*

---

*We've included a FREE one-hour online workshop titled *How to Handle the Greatest Challenge Every Entrepreneur Faces* as part of your Business Owner Fast Track Program. You can immediately access this video by going to **www.MauiMastermindBook.com**. See Appendix A for details.

working with David and the Maui team, I'd been fortunate enough to build a successful business (thisoldstore.com) and real estate portfolio that generated a seven-figure income. But I had to work long hours tied to my computer, phone, and email to do it—or so I thought.

"Using the Level Three approach, I've cut my working hours in half and still make the same income. Only now I don't come into the office until after 10 A.M., and I take every Friday off to be with my family for the weekend. This sure feels a lot more like wealth and freedom to me.

"For anyone who owns a successful business, I strongly recommend you use the Level Three business system to help you make it better. Who knows, you just might get your personal life back like I did."

The Powerful Perspective Shift Necessary to Build a Level Three Business

Making a critical shift in your perspective will enable you to build a Level Three business—and ultimately a Maui lifestyle. The switch is from seeing yourself as a *producer* for your business—driving sales and fulfilling client purchases—to seeing yourself as the *builder* of a business that will do all this without you. You're only a temporary producer until you can build the business that can replace you.

The Real Goal of Your Business:
To build a business that profitably creates
value in the market in a scalable way

Your business has to create value or no customers will hang around; it has to be profitable or it won't be sustainable. But it also has to be scalable or it will always be limited by you, the owner. If you have to be there to manage and run the enterprise, it can't expand to become a Level Three business. Yes, you can make a ton of money actively running a business, but why not make the money *and* have the freedom?

Now, we don't want to make building a Level Three business seem easy because it's not. While it may be simple when you know how, it will take work, sacrifice, and a deep commitment. But that initial effort directed to building an enterprise that can consistently create and deliver profitable value without you there to run the show is well worth it.

Stephanie's Story

A few years ago, my husband Jack and I took a five-week trip to Italy themed around fine wines and foods. We toured vineyards, took cooking classes, and visited cultural and historic sites throughout Italy.

When we came home, we met with our management team. After they brought us up to speed on the status of key projects and strategic initiatives, they shooed us out the door of the conference room, saying in effect, "We're fine. When is your next trip so we can get back to work?" That day, Jack and I realized we had succeeded in building a Level Three business. Our team didn't need us present to operate effectively. In fact, they loved having us gone because that meant they could spread their wings and take more ownership of the process of growing the business.

The 7 Major Benefits of Taking Your Business to Level Three

It's well worth investing your time, energy, and resources to build a thriving Level Three business. When you do, here are the seven tangible benefits you'll get:

1. **It gives you control over your financial future.** No matter what economic conditions you face, you have the financial strength that allows you to make the choices you want for you and your family. Plus, you

David's Story

I started my first "real" business at age 23 when I dropped out of college to start distributing a nutritional product in San Diego, California. Until then, I was a semi-professional athlete training for the Olympics. (I played on the United States National Field Hockey Team for seven years.) I was excited, ambitious, and ready to take on the world. That was until nine months later when I went bust!

(continued)

David's Story (continued)

What happened? I'd jumped into a business I didn't understand and didn't have a real passion for. I hadn't even bothered to write out a business plan. I'd never invested the energy to learn the skills needed to build a successful business. I was simply chasing after the glitter of easy profits.

That was my wake-up call.

They say the first sign of progress is admitting you have a problem—and boy, did I have a problem! I was scared, overwhelmed, and feeling stuck. I didn't understand how to sell or market; I had no skill in how to structure or run a business; and I had no clue how to manage cash flow and build financial controls! I had let my ego-fed pride blind me to my own ignorance and isolate me so I didn't look for the right mentors, advisors, and peer group to guide me.

Going bust helped me to break through my fear-based bravado and understand that I had a lot to learn. And learn I did. I studied. I read. I experimented. I found mentors to teach me and partners to contribute their best talents. I paid attention and focused on learning the key skills that had eluded me the first time around.

The result? Seven years later, I was an "overnight" success—a multimillionaire with two successful companies and a bright entrepreneurial future ahead of me.

But now I had another problem—a serious problem. I was totally burned out and overwhelmed. I was working 60- to 70-plus hours a week with lots of travel and meetings. And if that weren't enough, I was in danger of losing my passion for the business because of all the "details" I was responsible for overseeing.

Sure the money was great, but this wasn't what I'd signed up for. I originally started my own company because I wanted to be in control of my own destiny. I didn't want to work for anyone else (that is, if anyone else would've had me!). But in the end, I wanted one thing more than anything else. In fact, this one thing was the single deep desire that had sparked me to open up shop. It's what drove me to keep going when tough times hit.

I wanted *freedom*! Freedom from people telling me what to do and how to do it. Freedom to do things my way. Freedom from having my future depend on the whims or decisions of others. And—gulp—*time* freedom.

(continued)

David's Story (continued)

Instead of constantly working to feed my business and feeling trapped, I wanted to let my business work for me. The cash flow was great, but I always had to anticipate the pressures of the following month, with its payroll, overhead, necessary sales, and "emergencies" I knew I'd have to handle.

I wanted out of the pressure cooker, to escape the long hours and demands. Was it too much to ask for my business to support me instead of me working to support it?

It was at that point I made a decision. I'd build a business that would work without my showing up each day. I focused on it, obsessed over it, took action on it. And little by little, my business started to mature. I found key team members, built strong operational systems, and outsourced much of the day-to-day work.

What happened? Over the next 36 months, my income skyrocketed, but best of all, my free time kept pace. I had reduced my working hours to an average of 35 hours a week and increased my vacation time to two to three months a year. I was doing the things in the business that I loved out of choice, not obligation, because I'd crafted a role for myself in the company that was both sustainable and enlivening.

At this high point, I got such a good offer to sell the companies, I decided to do it. I took the money—along with everything I'd learned about building a successful business—and started fresh.

It was then that I realized the most exciting thing of all. The methodology I'd spent years developing to build a Level Three business worked even better the second and the third time around! I've used it for more than a decade in my various businesses. I've taught it to tens of thousands of entrepreneurs from around the world. And I know it will work for you if you just follow the map in this book.

have the security that comes from having mastered the skill of how to build a Level Three business. Should something happen to one of your businesses, you have the skills and experience to build another one.

2. **It will massively increase your net worth.** The average Level Three business is 10 times more valuable than its Level Two counterpart. Often your business will grow in value *one hundredfold or more* when you take it from Level Two to Level Three.

3. **Your business is much easier to scale.** By its very nature, a Level Three business is much easier to scale. It can easily accommodate

growth of 50 percent, 100 percent, or more—*per year!* One of our past Maui Advisors grew one of his Level Three businesses from $10 million to over $100 million in sales in 24 months!

4. **You earn your freedom from your business.** It no longer depends on your presence every day to make it work. You have many more options available to you. You get to do the parts of the business you're best at and love most, while letting other people handle the parts you don't enjoy.

5. **A Level Three business gives your staff security and growth opportunities.** The business isn't vulnerable to something happening to you, the owner. And as you grow the business and reduce its reliance on your daily presence, you give your staff opportunities to grow and develop as business people as they take on expanded roles in a vibrant, growing enterprise.

6. **Your business is dramatically more stable.** You're no longer vulnerable if one of your key team members—including yourself—gets hurt or has a life change.

7. **You have a greater impact on your market.** Because it's now scalable, your business is able to create more value for your market as it sells and delivers your products or services to your customers and clients. These products or services improve many people's lives.

Why Do You Want a Level Three Business?

It's been said that with a big enough *why*, you'll always be able to figure out the *how*. We invite you to step back and get clear on *your* why for building a successful business. What would it mean to you if your business were a Level Three business? What would the freedom of owning a Level Three business give you time to pursue? How would you be able to contribute more? What would be the biggest benefit to your family? How would it improve the lives and futures of your employees, vendors, and clients?

Action Time: What are the three strongest drives for you to invest the time, energy, and money to take your business to Level Three? In other words, looking back over your answers and thinking deeply, what are your three biggest reasons you'll do what it takes to grow your business to Level Three? Name them here.

1. _____

2. _____

3. _____

The 4 Most Costly Business Owner Myths

Myth 1: It's too risky.

We've heard it; you've heard it. *Starting your own business is too risky and 90 percent of new businesses fail within the first five years.* It's almost enough to scare you into taking another job with the nearest large, stable, "safe" company you can find (if, in fact, such a company exists).

But is starting your own business *really* so risky? Let's look at the facts.

Fact: According to most credible government and academic studies, a generic business start-up that has at least one employee has a roughly 70 percent chance of still being in business after two years (the way most studies define "success" for a start-up business). More than 50 percent are still in business after five years. And these numbers are misleadingly low in most instances. Why? Because the data doesn't account for businesses that close for legitimate reasons other than "business failure"—reasons such as health issues, the desire to start a new business, or other personal reasons.

We believe these statistics are a source of encouragement. After all, if 70 percent of new business owners can succeed through the first two years and at least half make it through year five, imagine how much better your odds are when you tap into the support, training, and input from resources such as the Maui community, local business groups, and online business networks.*

In our experience, most of the new businesses that fail do so because the business owner has no clear model, few skills, no mentors and advisors, and an inadequate support system. It's not the businesses that fail them; they fail their businesses because they don't invest the time and energy in *themselves* as owners. They work hard, but they work hard at the wrong things. They work at the job of doing their business, not at their role as a business owner.

Hard work is never enough; you've got to do the *right* work hard. When you develop your skills and community as a business owner, your

---

*We've created a comprehensive list of the key websites and resources you can tap into to help you reach your goals of building a Level Three business. We've made that list available for you at **www.MauiMastermindBook.com**.

odds of success rise dramatically. In fact, skilled entrepreneurs commonly have track records in the 80 to 90 percent success zone! They regularly move from one successful venture to another.

Besides, when you're told that someone says owning your own business is too risky, they're implying that working in a job is oh so much more "secure." Tell us, though; in your experience, is working for someone else really such a safe bet in today's world? We've all met people who've gone through wave after wave of layoffs and corporate restructurings. There's no guarantee of longevity in corporate life any more. We believe that when you master the skill of building a successful business, you're in the safest place of all.

David's Story

A close friend who worked for AOL Time Warner was laid off after 10 years and replaced by a new hire at half her salary and benefits. She'd invested more than 10 years of her working life there, all the while thinking that her diligence and commitment would keep her safe through retirement 40 years later. The world just doesn't work that way anymore. Working for a Fortune 500 company is no guarantee of stability.

The bottom line? Owning your own business does have risks, but the degree of control you have over your future—and the success rate for building your dream life—is magnitudes better than being trapped working for someone else.

Myth 2: It will consume your life.
Yes, launching a new business is intense. So are the Level Two years of establishing, grooming, and growing your company. But when you understand the Level Three Road Map, you see that as you grow your company, you not only can but *must* build it to be increasingly less dependent on you.

How you do your business life mirrors how you live your values in general. If you let your business crowd out all the other areas of your life, then regardless of the dollars you earn, you're still living an impoverished life.

Case Study: Stephen

One 7-year business owner client of ours recently shared this letter with us on how he has come to terms with the challenge of keeping his business in perspective:

"I've been guilty of losing perspective about where business fits into my life. For me, the danger points come when I've enjoyed big business success or I'm struggling with painful business failure. It's at these extremes that I've let business be too important in my life.

"At the high points of success, my pride and ego tempt me to bask in the approval and admiration of others. At the low points of failure, my need to succeed pushes me hard so I try to succeed by brute force and sheer will. But if 20 years in business have taught me anything, it's that I am not my businesses—not their successes nor their failures.

"When I'm at my best, living my deeper truth, I remember that my highest values start with faith, then family, and finally as a distant third, business."

Again, the bottom line is to build a business, not a job. Yes, it will be all-consuming early on, but over time you can transition your business away from needing you on a daily basis. This magical shift gives you *freedom*.

Myth 3: You've got to stay in control.
Control is a trap that will wrap your business around you, making it grow progressively more dependent on you. Instead, learn to build your business with the systems, team, controls, and scalable solutions in place that enable it to operate independent of your autocratic control. The more you build for personal control, the more you're trapped into being there daily to exercise that control and to personally run your business.

If all decisions and key actions must come back through you, then you become the single greatest bottleneck inside your own business. What's more, you don't have a business, you have a self-employed job. While this may satisfy some, don't settle for it. You *can* have more.

Level Three is a viable and realistic choice for you, but one you'll never enjoy if you cling to the fool's gold of building your business to maximize your personal control.

Myth 4: It takes a lot of money to launch a new business.
This is one of the most common and damaging misconceptions about launching your own business.

Fact: According to studies, most new businesses are launched with less than $10,000 of start-up capital. One study from Wells Fargo conducted by the Gallup Organization found that 73 percent of new businesses were launched with no outside funding of any kind and that the average business start-up used less than $10,000 of launch capital. While most new business owners wish they had more money at the start, by keeping their expenses to a minimum and being creative, they're able to launch their companies on a small amount of money—making launching a new business accessible to almost anyone. Of course, some businesses do require large capital outlays (usually for expensive equipment, extensive facilities, development costs, or required staffing), so these new business owners must raise outside funding.

Fact: If you require outside funding, you can bootstrap (fund out of sales), raise private capital (from family, friends, angel investors, or venture capital sources), borrow through SBA (Small Business Administration) loan programs, or create a joint venture to launch your business without a lot of *personal* capital.

A hundred years ago, it did take quite a bit of capital to establish a new business. But technology has changed the playing field, giving the newcomer easier and less expensive access to the great game of business than at any other time in history. And the trend is accelerating. Never before has it been easier and less expensive. So don't let lack of funding stop

David's Story

I launched my first successful business with $7,600. In fact, I launched it with $7,600 I didn't even have! That sum was my half of the start-up capital for a real estate training company I teamed up with a successful investor to build.

At the time, I was a 27-year-old athlete with no track record or relevant experience in business. My partner paid for his half out of his significant bank balance. I had to fund my half with credit cards. (Yes, I had to spread the $7,600 over two credit cards to cover my half.)

Within 90 days of launching our business, I'd recouped all my start-up capital and had a small, positive cash flow. Within 36 months, I was

(continued)

David's Story (continued)

pulling in a six-figure net profit. Within five years, I was making in the seven figures. All this was possible because I swallowed my fears and accessed this common source of outside capital—my credit cards—to fund my business. That original $7,600 investment grew into a $10 million business in less than seven years!

I have a question for you: What would you say to someone who said they couldn't come up with $7,600 to launch a business that seven years later would be worth millions?

You'd call them crazy. More important, you'd know that the lack of money was actually a lack of belief. If they *truly believed* in the opportunity and their ability to execute it, they would *find a way* to borrow or raise the money.

About 80 percent of the time the money issue comes up around launching a new business, I think it's just an excuse. That leaves 20 percent of the time when businesses *do* require larger amounts of capital to launch than the would-be founder has easy access to. But even in these cases, if the business idea, plan, and team are strong enough, the entrepreneur will find a way to raise the required start-up capital.

Remember, in life you can either buy your excuses or buy your dreams—but you can't buy both.

you from launching your dream business. You can and will find a way to access the capital you need.*

---

*We know that one of the most essential subjects for new business owners is exactly how to raise their start-up capital. That's why we created a FREE online workshop called *The 7 Sources to Secure Your Start-Up Capital*. It covers who to go to when you're looking for funding and how to "pitch" your deal to get them to say yes. For instant access to this workshop, go to **www.MauiMastermindBook.com**. See Appendix A for details.

CHAPTER 2

The Traditional Way of Building a Business versus the Level Three Road Map

The traditional way to build a business is to build a Level Two business. In a Level Two business, you as the business owner gather up the reins of power. All decisions are run past you. You create the plan, you lead the execution of that plan, you do all the hiring. You meet with all the key clients and perform most of the important work of the business. Sure, you have people to help, but they're there to do just that—help—not to lead or take ownership of central parts of your business. The core knowledge of how to manage and direct it is locked up in the gray matter of your brain. If something should happen to you, your business would crumble. If you manage to somehow escape for a short vacation, you probably sneak your laptop or iPhone® with you on the trip and check email when your spouse and kids aren't looking.

What's the real reason typical Level Two business owners want all the control? It's the fear that if they don't stay in control, things will go wrong. They're afraid that their staff will screw up and they'll lose a customer or face a lawsuit, or even that the company will fail. So they clutch at the security blanket of control, never seeing that it binds them in a trap that holds them in their businesses forever.

Remember the scene in *Godfather III* in which Michael Corleone (played by Al Pacino) wants to get out of the family business? He turns to his sister Connie and says, "Just when I thought I was out, they pull me back in!" Well, that's exactly how many Level Two business owners feel over time.

While there is nothing wrong with the traditional model, and it works to build a successful Level Two business, it has three serious pitfalls to it.

The 3 Pitfalls of Building Your Business the Level Two Way

Pitfall 1: It caps your income and your success. If your business revolves around you and your personal production, as you become more successful, you'll smack up against the ceiling of how much you personally are able to produce for your business. You can personally only do so much and run so fast before you just can't do any more.

Pitfall 2: It puts *everyone* at greater risk. If you stop working or get injured, your business dies—quickly. This is risky for you, your family, your employees, your customers, and your investors.

Pitfall 3: It eventually corners you in the Self-Employment Trap™— the more success you have, the more trapped you become inside your business. You're so busy doing the "job" of your business that you can't step back and focus on growing your business. As you grow your sales by personally producing more, you take on increasingly more overhead. That means each month, your starting point requires you to run even faster just to cover your fixed costs. It traps you firmly inside the suffocating blanket of your Level Two business.

So what's the way out of the Self-Employment Trap? Simple: build a business, not a job.

In the traditional Level Two approach, you try to escape by personally working harder. But that's like stepping on a treadmill and saying that the way to get off is to simply run faster. Not so. The faster you run, the faster the speed of the treadmill. You take on more overhead and hire more employees, but you put them into a Level Two model that merely increases your personal pressure to produce. And what happens if you ever stop running? You come crashing off the treadmill and your business dies.

You've got to build more than just a job; you've got to build a business.

Escaping the Self-Employment Trap

A job is something that you do *yourself*; a business you build does your job for you! Getting your business to do more means building the infrastructure that profitably produces value in the market in a scalable way.

This means building your business with the end in mind, the end being the day when it no longer needs your time and attention on a daily basis. In fact, building a Level Three business is a lot like raising kids. Immediately after birth and for the first few years, you put in a tremendous amount of care and feeding, not to mention changing a few diapers! This requires lots of your time.

In the early years of your business, you're naturally the main engine driving your business forward. You'll wear all the hats at various times, and you'll have few formal structures and systems within your organization upon which you can truly rely. But as it matures—like when your kids start school—you create some breathing space. You're confident you'll generate enough consistent sales that your business stays profitable.

As you enter Level Two, you'll face a crucial decision point at which you can settle for owning a Level Two job or instead choosing to raise your business to be a strong and independent entity that benefits from your involvement but is ultimately independent of it. Just like your goal as a parent is raising kids who can eventually stand on their own—independent and self-supporting—so your goal is to create an organization with the systems, team, controls, and scalable solutions that allow it to stand on its own.

The traditional Level Two approach is for you the owner to work harder, to do more—to work at the *job* of your business.

The Level Three solution is for you to do *less* and get your business to do more. Remember, the more you do, the more you have to keep doing! The more you get your business to do, the less you have to personally do, freeing up your time to grow and build your business.

The 4 Building Blocks of All Level Three Businesses

Every Level Three business is made up of these four key building blocks:

1. Systems
2. Team
3. Controls
4. Scalable solutions

Let's look at each of these four elements in turn.

Systems: The Backbone of Your Level Three Business

Systems are reliable processes and procedures that empower your business to consistently produce an excellent result for your clients or customers. They're documented best practices that increase your company's efficiency and reduce costly mistakes. Systems include documents and processes such as: the checklists your shipping clerks follow to ensure that all orders are shipped correctly; the orientation process for all new clients when you begin working together; and the standardized contracts you use with all your new hires and vendors. Basically, business systems include anything captured in a tangible format versus locked in the brain of an individual team member that enables the business to obtain consistently great results.

Case Study: Bonnie

One of our consulting clients,* Bonnie, owns a successful occupational therapy business in North Carolina. She's smart and a very talented occupational therapist. After we'd been working together for four months, it became clear that the office manager running the administrative and billing side of her business wasn't the right fit for her practice. It's never easy to let a team member go, but Bonnie knew her company needed someone else in that key role. It took her almost two months to gather her courage and break the news to this staff member. During that time, Bonnie realized that most of the knowledge for how to run the back office in her practice wasn't formally captured in any systems but existed in her own head as well as the head of this office manager. We coached Bonnie on how best to let her office manager go and use her new hire as an opportunity to systematize the core functions of that role.

Bonnie wrote a clear job description with the aim to hire to meet its requirements. She wrote out the step-by-step procedures for bringing on a new client, including collating all new client

---

*Many of the business owners you read about in this book are clients in our consulting program. Each quarter, we select a limited number of business owners to work with directly to take their businesses to Level Three. If you would like to find out more about this highly successful program, go to **www.MauiMastermindBook.com** and click on the "Consulting Program" link or see Appendix B for details.

documentation with filled-out samples so any team member could walk a new client through the process. She redesigned her billing procedures to make sure clients were charged the right amounts at the right times. She documented the therapist scheduling processes and the other key back-office functions. In the end, Bonnie reduced her business's reliance on any one person in the office manager's role, and she improved performance by creating clear systems and training her new hire on the systems. Not only that, she increased her cash flow by more than $50,000 by correcting all the mistakes in her practice's billing, which she painfully learned her old office manager had done inconsistently and haphazardly.

How much of your business know-how is locked away in the brains of others? What if you lose one or more of these team members? What can you do in the next 90 days to reduce your business's vulnerability if any of them were to leave, including you?

The Discipline of Creating Systems

Building systems is a team effort and a discipline. You'll need to train your team to create, organize, use, fine-tune, and if need be, eliminate your business systems. Many of your new team members will have little or no training in the importance, creation, and refinement of systems. In fact, some will see systems as a hassle or an impediment. It's your job to help them recognize how useful systems can be to get their jobs done — and how critical they are to the long-term success of the business. One of your key responsibilities is to establish the discipline and culture of creating and using systems in your organization.

You won't set this up all at once; rather, it's a cumulative process that takes place over time. We'll come back to this process again in more detail throughout this book. For now, we simply want to introduce you to the need for systems and to prime you to look at your business through a systems-reliant filter. It's our intention to spark in you the desire to no longer settle for one-off efforts of yourself or key employees, but instead establish system-driven solutions.

The 2 Layers to Every Successful Business System

Every successful business system has two layers: the process layer and the format layer. The *process layer* consists of the step-by-step process or procedure you've created. Does your system accurately capture the steps of the process so that when you follow it, you consistently get the desired result? It does you no good to formalize poor processes. You want your systems to capture your best practices and winning moves, making it easier for your company to replicate and scale those successes.

The *format layer* deals with how you package and present your system to your team. Is your system easy to use? Is it transparent so team members intuitively understand how to use it? Can it be automated so much of the work happens via technology instead of manual work? For example, this could be automated reporting built into your database to track sales or monitor client orders. It could also be enterprise software that your team uses to run the entire flow of your business, featuring key systems built directly into the software. Or it could be simple, low-tech tools like a script for your scheduling assistant to use when he or she leaves a message for people, or a standardized form that your receptionist gives each new client to fill out upon arriving for an appointment.

Done right, systems make life easier for your team and success more predictable for your business.

A Simple Test to Know If You Got Your System's Format Correct

Having a solid process isn't enough. You have to package that process in ways that your team will actually use.

How do you know if your system has a good, useable format?

Ask one simple, unambiguous, incontrovertible question: *Is your team using it?* The real test is whether your team embraces it, ignores it, or even worse, creates a shortcut system for the task.

Your team members want to do a good job. If your business systems are simple, intuitive, and effective, they will use them. If they're confusing, complicated, bloated, or cumbersome, they'll ignore these systems and even create their own "cheat sheet" hybrid versions instead. But these homespun, individual hybrids normally aren't scalable. In fact, they usually only work for that one team member and only as long as the volume of your business stays relatively level. Plus, even if this private shortcut works, rarely is it ever captured in a way that the rest of your business can use it. And when that team member goes, so does that know-how.

To get the format layer right, watch the way your team members use, or don't use, your systems. Don't argue, don't preach, don't cajole—simply observe. Take their behavior as critical feedback to refine and improve your systems. Remember, they're meant to leverage, empower, and simplify the lives of your employees, so don't fall in love with any specific system. Rather, fall in love with the result it's intended to generate.

25 Effective Formats to Package Your Systems

Here is a quick list of 25 potential formats for you to package your systems to make them easier and more effective for team members to use.

1. Checklists
2. Scripts
3. Worksheets
4. Step-by-step instructions
5. Software that automates a process
6. Databases of key information
7. Pricing lists
8. Templates and samples
9. Common Q & A sheets
10. Written "warnings" for an area, providing how to deal with predictable problems
11. Spreadsheets with built-in formulas
12. Camera-ready artwork
13. Filing system (paper or electronic)
14. Preapproved vendors lists
15. Standardized equipment and parts
16. Online communication tools for effectively sharing information (discussion forums, wikis, whiteboards, social networks, etc.)
17. Delivery timetables
18. Job descriptions
19. Instructional videos
20. Project management software with reusable project pathways
21. Reporting templates
22. Organizational charts
23. Pre-approved forms and contracts
24. A timeline or Master Calendar
25. Complete enterprise management software

Team: The Leverage Point to Enroll the Unique Talents of Other People

Every business needs talented people to help make it successful. Our insistence that your business's success be independent of any one person does *not* mean your team is unimportant. On the contrary, the only way to build a Level Three business is to have great team members who consistently perform for your company. It's critical, however, to ensure that it doesn't rely on the presence of any one individual. Instead, capture critical know-how in your systems. Make key team members responsible for creating the systems to do their individual jobs and groom their successors.

Your goal is to empower your people to use their talents and abilities to help the business as a whole get great results. Therefore, aim to enlist your team to leverage the *business* and not merely to leverage *you*, the owner. You're not looking to be the star yourself; you're striving to build a business that attracts and empowers stars.

Paying for Top Talent

Many business owners worry about the cost of hiring new staff, especially bringing on high-order team members to run specific areas of the company. We understand. In running dozens of businesses, we've dealt with the scary thoughts of hiring new team members and taking on the additional fixed overhead of their salaries and benefits. Done right, though, all your new hires will result in a net positive cash flow for your business. In fact, if you don't see how a new hire will increase the bottom line, you're not making the right hire.

Don't be afraid to bring on talented leaders to help you grow your business. Of course you need to be prudent and ensure your business can afford the increase in overhead. But the right hires will yield you a return of many times their cost.

David's Story

I remember the first key hire I made for one of my businesses—a chief operating officer (COO) named Paige. Factoring in her salary, benefits, and indirect expenses, the cost was roughly $100,000 a year. At the time, this was a huge leap of faith for me because the business was bringing in only about $1 million a year in sales.

(continued)

> ### David's Story (continued)
>
> Before hiring her, my partner and I were conducting all the sales and marketing *and* overseeing all the operations. But we hated the detailed routine of the operational area. It drained us. What's more, we weren't great at it. By bringing on Paige, we got a world-class COO to completely take over operations, which freed up hours of our time every week. We reinvested this time in growing our sales and creating new products.
>
> In the first 12 months, we grew our sales from $1 million to $3 million! What's more, the next year we grew our sales to $6 million. None of this would have been possible if we hadn't hired Paige. Not only did she free up our time to grow the business, but she was vastly superior at running the operational side than we were. She actually loved the disciplined details needed to run operations.
>
> Before we brought Paige on board, both my partner and I subconsciously resisted growing fast. Frankly, we feared what large-scale growth would require of us. Hiring Paige eliminated that fear. She built out the core operational systems and helped us staff up to accommodate explosive growth. Most important, she reinforced the need and rewards for bringing talented leaders into our business. So when we brought on our chief financial officer, chief marketing officer, chief sales officer, and chief technology officer, we were more comfortable with the need for these roles and the added payroll demands.

Controls: Intelligent Checks and Balances That Put Your Business in Control (Not You)

As mentioned earlier, most business owners build their companies to maintain—and even expand—their personal control over every aspect of the business. However, this traditional way ends up trapping you at Level Two.

Think of it this way. *You* don't need to be in control; you need your *business* to be in control. What's the difference? When you are in control, you need to be present daily to exercise that control. When your business is in control, it operates with a solid foundation of systems, processes, and procedures to address the *business's* needs, not just your fears and limitations as the owner.

Controls are the intelligent processes, procedures, and safeguards that protect your company from uninformed or inappropriate decisions or actions by any team member. When you build a business versus a job, you want your team to have the authority to get tasks done without running everything past you. Just make sure you have safeguards in place to protect the business.

For example, to reduce the potential for embezzlement, you would have one person make deposits and a different, unrelated person reconcile your bank statements. This is an example of a sound financial control.

Or you might formalize how you give team members levels of decision-making authority that aligns with their experience and the degree of consequence if they decide poorly.

Or you might institute weekly reporting of key indicators that help your team monitor performance and trends and proactively respond to changes in your business. These are all examples of business controls and we'll give you more, but for now, the bottom line is this: *The more you build your business for control, the more you are trapped inside your business.*

A Common Question That Could Lead You Astray
During a small-group mastermind session for our consulting clients, Cheryl asked an interesting question about growing her business.

Before sharing her question and the answer we gave, here's a bit of context: Cheryl had built a successful Middle Stage Level Two business with two locations and a steady stream of clients. (Later in the book, we'll break down Level Two into three stages: Early, Middle, and Advanced. For now, what matters most is that a Level Two business works, but only if the owner is present to make it work.) Like most business owners, Cheryl was dealing with the challenges of delegation. Here's how she stated the question:

"How do I delegate more and more of my day-to-day responsibilities to other people on my team and still maintain control of my business?"

In this simple question lies one of the greatest dilemmas you'll ever face. On one hand, you need to leverage your team to get more done by delegating. On the other hand, you want to maintain control so negative consequences don't ensue if team members drop the ball or do things the wrong way. But the solution isn't to choose either of these two options; instead, it requires reformulating the question. As it's stated, the question presupposes that you, the business owner, *should* maintain personal control of your business. That creates a false dilemma and if you fall prey to it, you'll lose both your freedom *and* your control over your business.

It's not a choice between *"delegate and lose control"* or *"hang onto things and keep the control."* Deciding between those two choices is counterproductive if you're committed to building a Level Three business. You can either react or respond to the issue of control. Here's the difference.

Control is a Level Two reaction:

- It's fear based.
- It's autocratic.
- It means you're gathering more and more of it for yourself versus the business.
- It says, *"Check with me"* and *"I'll make that decision each time it comes up"* and *"Don't take the next step until I look it over."*

Control*s* are a Level Three response:

- They're proactive.
- They're enterprise driven (building controls for your business, not for you, the owner).
- They're primarily tools to allow everyone in your business to see the status, check on results, and self-correct as needed.
- They say, *"Check the dashboard"* and *"Follow our internal process"* and *"How do we implement a systems-based control here?"*

So let's reformulate Cheryl's question this way: *"How can I build intelligent controls into my business to ensure that everything happens at the right time and in the right way so I am free to scale the business?"*

Case Study: Steve

Steve, a consulting program client, was the co-owner of a successful Advanced Stage Level Two business on the verge of going to Level Three. But he was being held back because he kept spending too much time managing the day-to-day details of the operational area of his company. He struggled with the idea that he could step away from that level of involvement without too many mistakes being made and his business suffering. He "got it" intellectually that he needed to extricate himself, but just couldn't swallow it emotionally.

After a few months of positive peer pressure from the other business owners in his mastermind group, he committed to "not pick up any piece of equipment" in his warehouse and get himself out of all day-to-day operations by year-end. (Don't *you* wish you had a peer group committed to take their businesses to Level Three and push you to do the same?) This was a *huge* breakthrough! Steve's business sells millions of dollars of computer parts every year. Each time he got involved in the fulfillment end of boxing, testing, or moving parts, it cost his business thousands of dollars in lost revenue. Why? Because it took Steve away from creating the sales systems that would sell more parts.

If checking orders and parts cost him so much money in lost sales, why did he insist on repeating that behavior for so long? Simple. He wanted to maintain control. Control is seductive; it tempts you to put yourself at the center of your business. Control is addictive; the more you insist on it, the more hooked you and your company become on relying on your stamp of approval every step of the way.

We're happy to report that while it took him 10 months to do it, Steve got himself out of the operational area of his business. He did it by weaning his operations team and systems off relying on him personally. He's now investing the 20-plus hours a week that he saved into building his sales force. He set a goal of increasing annual sales from $10 million to $30 million over the next 36 months. This wouldn't have been possible if he hadn't turned over the details of his company's operations to the systems he built and the team he trained.

35 Business Controls Most Businesses Need

Let's talk specifics. Here are 35 examples of business controls in five categories that most businesses will eventually need to get to Level Three.

As you read this list, understand that it isn't comprehensive—but it provides a sense of what we mean by business controls. Also, don't stress out thinking you need to build in all these controls *this quarter*. Accept that building in controls is a work in progress to be implemented over time.

Financial Controls

When it comes to the topic of "Control," no subject is more emotionally charged than financial controls. Business owners fear possible financial abuses and mistakes if they don't personally control the money in the business. This is shortsighted and costly thinking.

Take a look at 10 sound financial controls that are both scalable and powerful in protecting your enterprise from financial abuses. Again, the list is not comprehensive, but it provides a concrete sense of what controls look and feel like.

1. **Have more than one person involved in any one cycle of money.** This is an essential "check and balance." Having two or more people sign off on all money flows and money cycles reduces temptation and makes fraud or theft less likely. Here are a few examples:

   - Person A logs in checks and cash; person B verifies the math and makes the deposit.
   - Person A deposits the money; person B reconciles the bank statements.
   - Person A writes out the checks; person B reviews and signs them.

2. **Thoroughly check employees and independent contractors *before* you hire them.** Do a criminal background check on each one and, if they handle money in any form, a credit check, too. Verify employment history and talk with past references, confirming that these references are real.

3. **Reduce liquid cash, which is always a temptation.** Get cash out of the system ASAP and with great care and attention. Here are a few examples of what you can do:

   - Replace petty cash with a reimbursement system.
   - If an employee collects cash from a customer, have that cash immediately deposited the same day with two people involved in that cycle of money flow.
   - Get machines that take credit cards versus only coins and bills.

4. **Have appropriate balances accessible in operating accounts and keep other monies in a segregated account(s) with tighter financial controls.** This lowers your exposure yet allows you to give access to small accounts with appropriate controls to staff who need operating money.

5. **For purchasing decisions, formally set levels of spending authority for your team.** For example, if the expense is less than $1,000, no approval is needed, but supporting documentation and receipts must be filed with the area manager. If the expense is more than $1,000 but less than $5,000, the area manager must approve the expense in advance. If the expense is more than $5,000. . . . You get the idea.

6. **Establish formal refund and return policies that spell out who is and is not authorized to refund.** Spell out which kinds of refunds each has the authority to do.

7. **Determine safeguards for customer credit cards and other financial information.** For example, lock all file cabinets, shred trash daily, use password protection on computer databases.

8. **Create a formalized expensing system.** This would include a list of expenses that are and are not reimbursable as well as a standardized expense report team members must use. Include a space on that form for the person to sign, declaring the expenses submitted are true and accurate. Require that receipts be attached for all expensed items.

9. **Get to know your business and the key numbers so you can quickly see what's normal and what's not.** Encourage your management team to understand the same. Make it a core value of your business to immediately red flag anything that seems strange. Follow up on all red flags immediately. Here are some examples:

   - *Key ratios:* Check your cost of goods sold ratio, net income percentages, gross margins, and other relevant financial ratios for your business on a regular basis. These should stay consistent. If they vary or look abnormal, find out why.

   - *Key expenses:* If you don't recognize a vendor, suspect an expense is out of line, or see income anomalies, investigate immediately.

   - *Key rough checks:* Look at the indirect ways of ball-parking your financial numbers to corroborate that things are in line with what's normal. For example, compare inventory turns to sales figures; compare staff hours to sales volume; etc.

10. **Obtain the right kind of insurance and bonding coverage** if appropriate.

Operational Controls

11. **Manage costs and expenditures** with approved operating budgets.

12. **Manage client fulfillment** with production schedules and checklists of deliverables.

13. **Monitor client satisfaction** with follow-up surveys and informal interviews.

Marketing Controls

14. **Establish and follow a Master Marketing Calendar** that lays out key deadlines and review dates to make sure your marketing campaigns stay on track.

15. **Create visual scorecards for key marketing metrics.** For example, cost per lead; cost per sale; net leads per lead source; etc.

16. **Establish a formal approval process** for your quarterly marketing plan, creative artwork, and other key marketing output early in the process before you spend too much time or money on them.

17. **Have a checklist your team follows** when promoting an event or launching a marketing campaign.

Sales Controls

18. **List negotiating parameters your sales team can work within out in the field.** Examples might be pre-approved concessions your sales team can use to close a sale, discounts or credits your front-line staff are authorized to give when dealing with a purchasing customer in your store, and so on.

19. **Establish an approval process for sales exceptions.** For example, if a concession is worth less than $500, the sales manager must verbally approve it; if a concession exceeds that amount, the sales manager must physically sign off on it.

20. **Require standardized sales paperwork and contracts.**

21. **Provide sales team with formalized sales scripting.**

22. **Require employment contracts that protect the proprietary nature of your client list.** Possibly parcel out access to that database among the sales people so that they never have access to more of that list than they actually need.

23. **Require sales people to use only company-controlled contact phone numbers, emails, fax numbers, etc. with clients.** They should never be expected or allowed to give out personal contact information.

24. **Provide a direct line for client feedback** that doesn't allow sales people to filter out negative messages.

25. **Record clear and accurate sales metrics.** These would include closing ratios, retention rates, return rates, net referral score, and so on.

Metrics and Scorecards

A scorecard, sometimes called a "dashboard," is a simple visual way to measure how a key area of your business is performing. It's like looking up at the scoreboard of an athletic event and seeing the time remaining, the score of both teams, and who's got possession of the ball.

Quantitative data gives your entire team a simple, clear, objective way to measure the performance of an area of your business. If the numbers show you're off course, your scorecard can flash a yellow or red alert to your team so they can remediate the situation.

Here are examples of metrics your business may want to measure on its scorecards.

26. **Gross Margins.** [*(Total Sales – Cost of Sales) ÷ Total Sales*]

27. **Number of new leads into business per day, week, or month.**

28. **Cost per lead by lead source.** [*Total Number of Leads by Lead Source ÷ Total Cost of Generating those Leads by Lead Source*]

29. **Average unit of sale.** (*Total Gross Sales ÷ Total Number of Customer Orders*)

30. **Average time to process new orders.**

31. **Return rate by product category.**

32. **Defects per 1,000 parts.**

33. **On-time delivery rate.**

34. **Average number of days before you turn your inventory.**

35. **Actual expenses to budgeted expenses.**

You may be thinking that business controls sound like formalized business systems, and you're right! Every key control is, in reality, a defined, formalized business system so that "checks and balances" aren't left to chance but built into the structure of the business. This protects your company and allows you to have peace of mind, even when you let go of direct control over a process, action, or decision.

5 Quick Steps to Immediately Upgrade Your Current Business Controls

Here are five simple action steps for you to immediately upgrade your business's existing controls.

1. **Eliminate or amend wasteful controls you currently have in place.** Examples of wasteful business controls include: requiring

the business owner to sign off on all purchasing decisions no matter what the amount; requiring staff to generate reports that don't create value for the business or influence decisions of the management team; not allowing front-line employees to make simple decisions that thrill customers yet don't cost the business too much money. Stop for a moment now, and list possibly wasteful controls you currently have in place along with how you can eliminate or improve them.

2. **Review your** *financial* **controls, and (ideally) get a trained expert to help you easily upgrade them.** This can be your CPA or, if you have one, your CFO. The expert will look at the flow of money through your business and the danger points where your business needs stronger controls in place.

3. **Build a clear scorecard that makes it easy to see the score.** Do you have a metric in place to gauge performance in the key areas of your business? As best you can, have all key controls correlate to a key measurement, or "scorecard," so you can measure results at a glance and make any needed adjustments. A visual scorecard will help the people doing the work measure their performance and give management a tool to ensure your business is functioning optimally.

4. **Observe which of your current systems your team actually uses, and reformat, redesign, or eliminate the ones they don't use.** Remember, a business control is a subset of a business system, and a system in the wrong format is of no value, even if it could technically work. Observe your team's behaviors to see if your systems are functional. Behaviors don't lie. If a system is significant and technically accurate but isn't being used, tweak the *format* of the system to make it more user friendly.

5. **Push decisions down to the lowest level they can competently be made.** Nothing is more deadening for your team members than requiring them to go to you for decisions they are competent and fully informed to make. It kills initiative and arbitrarily creates a stifling bottleneck in your business—you! The more you personally must decide, the more you must keep on deciding. Your goal must be to create intelligent controls that allow your team to make decisions they are competent to make. But also put safeguards in place so big decisions get well thought out before it's too late to change them.

Scalable Solutions: Removing Barriers and Unnecessary Constraints

Have you ever watched the television show *This Old House*? Imagine you're on it, working on a 75-year-old house with its original electrical wiring and plumbing. What would happen if you plugged in a full complement of modern electrical appliances? You'd blow your fuses, not to mention create the potential for an electrical fire to break out. And what would happen to your plumbing if you went from a well-water system to tapping into the higher pressure of city water? (Can you say rain gear?!)

Likewise, too much growth that makes increasing demands on old, outdated systems is what causes most growing businesses to fail. The systems that worked for a $500,000-a-year business are no longer sufficient to cope with a $5 million business, and not even close to being adequate for a $50 million business. At first, the additional sales will cause a few "leaks," but before long, your business will have burst pipes and water everywhere! That's why the final building block of a Level Three business is scalable solutions.

Case Study: Morgan

Morgan was a young man in his late 20s when he started his mortgage brokerage company, Morgan Financial. He built a successful Level Two business for himself in Portland, Oregon. After a few years operating in one office, Morgan took the scary step of opening a second office. It turned out to be profitable, and for a time, he settled back enjoying the results of his two offices. If that were the end of Morgan's ambitions, the story would have ended like it does for most small-business owners . . . with Morgan settling back into his 30- to 40-year role of running his two-office mortgage business as a self-employed business owner.

And for years, that's the business he was satisfied with—two offices helping home buyers get mortgages. That was until he met a key mentor named Doug. About 10 years older than Morgan, Doug had built up several successful businesses. He provided the capital, confidence, and counsel that Morgan needed to scale his business to Level Three.

Over the next eight years, Morgan went from two offices with a handful of staff to more than 200 offices and 1,000 team members in 23 states doing $1 billion of loans annually. Morgan made the first leap from one to two offices by himself in four years. With the help of his mentor, he went from two to 200 offices—a one hundredfold increase—over the next eight years! How did Morgan explode his business from two to 200 offices in such a short time? He followed the Level Three Road Map and built a systems-reliant business with sound controls and a clear way of doing things that he and his team scaled rapidly.

Morgan and Doug ended up selling their company to a private equity firm and made millions because they actively understood and followed the Level Three Road Map.*

*Would you like to watch Morgan tell his full story, including the mistakes he made and the lessons he learned along the way? Simply go to **www.MauiMastermindBook.com** and watch this 25-minute video interview for FREE! See Appendix A for details.

Scaling your business requires building it in such a way that your model and systems can be rolled out and replicated on a much bigger playing field. This also means when you're solving a business challenge, you look for solutions that can be scaled. For example, imagine you're an online retailer who sells physical products online. One choice for shipping customer orders is for you to hire your cousin Vinny to come over each day to your garage and box and ship out your orders.

Vinny is an extreme example of an "unscalable" solution. You could improve the situation by hiring a full-time person to set up and run a formal in-house shipping department. This solution would be slowed by your need to hire more people and secure more space as you grow. Plus, you'd have to invest in the technology and develop the systems to cost-effectively monitor your inventory and do your shipping.

A third—and scalable—solution would be to outsource your shipping to a professional fulfillment company that already has thousands of times the capacity and proven systems to reliably ship your orders.

Take another example. Imagine you're building a web platform to process orders from your traveling sales force. When evaluating which platform to purchase, a Level Three thinker would choose one that could handle the high transaction volume you eventually want to have, provided the cost for this greater capacity isn't too high. If the cost doesn't make financial sense, consider a smart alternative. Choose a platform that can be easily upgraded later as your sales volume increases and you have the excess cash flow to warrant the upgrade. You'd say "no" to any platform that couldn't handle your expected sales volume or be easily upgraded and expanded later.

7 Examples of Scalable Solutions

Scalable solutions are flexible. They remove barriers to growth and eradicate unnecessary constraints. Here are seven examples of scalable solutions that business owners we've worked with have used to profitably scale their companies:

1. **Outsource inbound orders to a call center.** You not only benefit from the flexible staffing of the call center, but you get instant access to the systems and technology that the call center has developed to handle hundreds or thousands of times the call volume you may initially have.

2. **Create a new client "Quick Start" DVD or kit** that introduces new clients to the steps they need to know working with your business. Then a live staff person isn't required to constantly repeat the information.

3. **Build an online inventory control database** that automatically ties your sales data into your inventory control, accounting, and purchasing systems.

4. **Move from working with one client at a time to working with a group of clients.** For example, you could offer webinars and teach online classes to hundreds of clients at the same time with no added time and few additional costs. (Bonus: Make recordings of those classes available for later download by thousands of additional clients.)

5. **License a key piece of intellectual property (I.P.) to another company for a royalty.** You let them use their sales team and production capacity to market, sell, produce, and deliver a product or service using your I.P. in return for a regular royalty payment.

6. **Joint venture with a complementary company** to provide your customers with a new product or service to purchase and enjoy. No fulfillment or customer service would be necessary on your part.

7. **Create a hiring and new-team-member orientation system** that allows you to staff up quickly as your business grows.

David's Story

Many business owners say that because they're selling expertise that lives in their heads, they can't scale their businesses. We understand. Not only do many of our clients face this

(continued)

David's Story (continued)

challenge, but we also had to deal with the issue with our Maui Mastermind Consulting Program. Essentially we offer our clients a service that relies on expert knowledge and a sensitivity to each person's individual business situation and needs. So how did we make this scalable?

First, we processed out our methodology so that we could capture the expert knowledge of how we go about building a Level Three business into a clear, step-by-step system. Not only did this allow us to work with more business owners, but the time and focused attention we invested in this process helped us to refine it, so that our clients get more value and better results.

This is something too many business owners who have a business wherein they are selling their expertise don't realize—the very process of systematizing your expert way of doing something helps you to improve your expertise, both by refining your methodology and by improving how you implement, apply, and transfer that expertise to your clients.

Second, we created the internal controls necessary to make sure that our team is using our core coaching systems in the right way, at the right time. These include the checklists that our coaching team follow at various stages of a client's work with us, the scorecards that let our team know that clients are on track, and the defined processes that give our clients a consistently powerful experience. It is not enough to have sound systems, you need to have a timely way to ensure that your team is actually using your systems to get your clients the results they've hired you to help them get.

Third, we built into the program direct and intimate access to the Maui Advisors so that our clients get to work directly with business owners who have built Level Three businesses themselves, and can share out of their personal experiences. After all, how can someone take you to a place that he or she has never been? Most of the Maui Advisors initially started out as clients of ours and now participate as a way of "paying it forward" to the next generation of business owners. This means that the program itself is constantly grooming the next generation of Level Three business owners to step up into the role of Maui Advisor.

(continued)

David's Story (continued)

But we couldn't just start with this third element as we built the program because it wouldn't have been enough. It would have been too variable and chaotic. We needed to wrap this core element of direct access to Level Three business owners with a clear, step-by-step structure and the internal controls necessary to ensure that clients were getting great results.

In the end, by combining these three elements—systems, controls, and team—we can offer our clients something that no one else can: a proven road map to Level Three along with the accountability structure and expert input to guarantee that they get there.

Outsourcing: Leveraging Other Companies' Systems and Teams

One of the least understood tools available for growing your business is outsourcing. Outsourcing is when you take a function, activity, or need of your business and hire an outside company to do the work instead of doing it in-house. This includes: contracting with a fulfillment company to stock and ship all your customer orders; hiring an online marketing company to do your pay-per-click ad campaigns for you; turning over your payroll to a professional employment agency; and so on. It allows you to expand capacity *without* having to:

- formally hire large numbers of new staff;
- invest in new capital equipment or lease larger commercial space;
- invest in development costs for non-core parts of your business, increasing your fixed overhead.

4 Reasons Outsourcing Provides Great Leverage

1. **You get instant scale in that area of your business.** For example, the fulfillment company you hire already has the capacity to handle 100 times the order volume you currently have; the payroll service you use can immediately handle any increased staff you hire, etc.

2. **You get the benefit of all the development costs and trial-and-error learning that the outsourced service provider had to go through to build that business.** You skip all this and tap directly into a proven business system and team in that specialty area. In essence, the outsourced service provider has amortized all the significant development costs over its base of customers, of which you are one.

3. **Your outsourced service provider offers expertise your business lacks.** For example, the shipping and distribution company you outsource to may have decades of experience for what may be very new to you; the advertising agency has created hundreds of television ads before, whereas you may have only been involved in one or two, etc.

4. **As the outsourced provider grows and matures its business, you get immediate access to that company's upgrades in know-how, systems, and staff.**

3 Criteria to Determine When It's Smart to Outsource

1. **When outsourcing lowers your real cost.** Make sure you factor in the direct and indirect costs of keeping the work in-house as well as the direct and indirect costs of outsourcing the work. Indirect costs to keeping it in-house include: loss of staff time and focus to perform the work; increased overhead to both perform and manage the work; and more complexity for your business to manage. Indirect costs to outsourcing include: the cost to find and implement an outsourced solution; the cost to replace any failed outsourced relationship; and the costs to integrate the outsourced service with your own company systems.

2. **When outsourcing increases the value you provide your customers and clients.** For example, will outsourcing give you faster and more reliable delivery service for the same or less money? Will outsourcing give you access to better technology in this area than you could afford to buy or lease yourself?

3. **When the outsourced area or function isn't core to your business.** If the area or function you're outsourcing is the main way you create value in your business, then outsourcing puts you at risk. In fact, disruption in the outsourced solution can kill your business, leaving you vulnerable. While it can be appropriate to outsource a core area or function of your business, be much more cautious

about doing so. Do thorough due diligence on the service provider you hire. Make sure you have contingency plans in place to handle the worst-case scenario of the outsourced relationship failing.

David's Story

One important way Maui Mastermind communicates with the members of the Maui community is via email. Each month, we send close to a million emails to our community members sharing business tips, case studies, notice of upcoming events, and links to interesting video or audio blog posts. Initially, we housed our company database with a small third-party company that sent out our eletters for us. We'd send the eletter to Chris, the owner of this provider, along with the date we wanted him to email it to our clients, and he'd send it out on the appropriate date.

However, as you can imagine, this solution was rife with problems as we grew. First, if Chris got too busy with other work, he might send out our eletters late, and many of the eletters contained time-sensitive information! Any late eletters also threw off our entire client communication calendar. Also, if we needed to make a last-minute change to the eletter, such as fix a link or update an announcement, we'd have to rush an email to him and call him in a panic. If we didn't reach him before he pushed that send button, we were out of luck. Worst of all, his system required him to manually maintain our client list's integrity to make sure our eletters got delivered. Obviously, this was not a highly scalable solution.

So we researched alternatives and found a web-based email platform and database solution that would allow us to do everything that Chris did for us, plus do it for a client list 100 times the size! We also reduced the steps needed to successfully send out eletters, simplified the process of managing our client list, and got instant access to templated performance reporting built into this new service. And if that weren't enough, because we were one of a number of clients using this service, we benefited from the system upgrades they constantly came up with to make their service better. All this for a small monthly fee roughly equivalent to what we paid Chris when we hired his small company to provide the same service.

The heart of finding scalable solutions is to look for choices that remove barriers to growth. In this case, the constraint was in our email communication, but it could just as easily have been with our need to scale live event production or our online workshops or any one of a number of other business functions.

4 Strategies to Help You Scale Your Business

1. **Upgrade your clients.** Too many business owners are satisfied working with the same level of clients for too long. Scale up the level of clients so you work with larger contracts, projects, and client relationships. Done right, in most businesses this will increase net income because selling costs as a percentage of sales volume go down—and many times your costs to fulfill on the product or service will also go down as you take advantage of economies of scale.

   Quickly, list five potential clients you'd love to land—ones that would instantly increase your business volume by 25, 50, or even 100 percent. What would be your first step to cultivate them as a client or customer?

   ### Case Study: Windswept Marketing, Inc.

   One of the companies we work with in our consulting program, Windswept Marketing, Inc., sells specialty items such as branded key chains and embroidered shirts. For several years, their average client purchased $4,000 to $6,000 worth of products each year. Then last year, Windswept landed its first "mega" client—Home Depot. The first year Windswept had Home Depot as a client, it increased sales by $300,000, effectively doubling sales with *one* new client. Now Windswept is pursuing five more mega-clients, any one of which has the potential of increasing sales by 50 to 100 percent!

2. **Scale up your project size.** If your business normally focuses on $50,000 projects, consider what it would take to go after projects $100,000 to $250,000 in size. This requires a stretch, but it's an incredible leverage point for your business. We'll let you in on this little secret: It takes proportionately less energy to do a project 5 or 10 times larger than you've done in the past than it does to do 5 or 10 more smaller-sized projects. This means that taking on larger projects will usually result in more profits from less time and effort.

   What's your average project size? Brainstorm five ways you could scale up your project size to do projects that are 5 to10 times bigger. Then choose one idea from this list to apply to your business.

Case Study: Maui Advisor Bill Shopoff

Twenty years ago, Maui Advisor Bill Shopoff launched his real estate investment company by buying and fixing up distressed single-family residences and reselling them for a profit. He worked full time and long hours to build a successful investment company, which back then, focused on deals worth a few hundred thousand dollars each.

Fast forward to today. Bill and his team currently look for $20 million or larger projects. He's scaled up his target project size by a hundredfold! Currently Bill's company, The Shopoff Group, employs a team of savvy real estate professionals who've helped Bill buy and sell more than $1 billion of real estate. Bill scaled his business mostly by taking on much larger projects.*

———————————

*Would you like to watch Bill tell his full story, including how he went from a personal bankruptcy and living on the couch of a friend for over three months to becoming one of the top commercial real estate investors in the county? Simply go to **www.MauiMastermindBook.com** and watch this 40-minute video interview FREE! It's an inspirational story that will touch you deeply (especially when he shares about his relationship with his wife Cindy). See Appendix A for details.

3. **Scale up your winning sales and marketing systems.** The key word here is winning. It does you no good to scale up your mediocre efforts. However, this approach requires you to have accurate numbers tracking your sales and marketing efforts. If you don't, tracking systems and a meaningful sales and marketing scorecard is the place for you to start.

Assuming you know which sales and marketing systems are your clear winners, brainstorm 10 ways you could scale them up. Could you send a winning direct mail letter to more people? Could you bring on more commissioned sales team members? Could you increase your key word ad buy? Could you focus on scaling up your affiliate program? You get the idea.

Take the energy that you invest in your poorest performing 50 percent of sales/marketing systems and redirect that considerable time, money, and focus on your winners.

4. **Scale up your fulfillment capacity.** With respect to scaling up your fulfillment capacity, let's make a very important point. We

don't mean to just staff up. Depending on your business, this may be the best *or* the worst thing you could ever do.

Every business has to balance its ability to market and sell with its operational capacity to fulfill on the products and services sold. This dynamic balance is rarely ever perfectly aligned. Staffing up for many businesses means increasing fixed overhead dramatically, with little flexibility to accommodate for fluctuations in sales or cash flow. This can kill a growing business that experiences a temporary lull.

Instead, we suggest you scale your fulfillment systems to handle more volume while adding little fixed overhead. You can do this by developing better workflow processes and efficiencies that allow your existing team to produce more. Your company can become more efficient by developing outsourced vendors to use for non-core work as needed. Or you can invest in the technology to leverage your existing team and resources.

The key question to ask is this: *How can I dramatically increase my fulfillment capacity without taking on more fixed overhead?* Take a moment and list five ways you could do this.

Beware the Naysayers

While all this talk about scaling your business to Level Three sounds great in theory, we know the world is full of naysayers who will tell you it can't be done. They'll say the only way to build a business is through hard work and long hours. They'll tell you it just isn't possible for you to build a Level Three business. (Ironically, many of these naysayers are people who actually work for Level Three businesses! But hey, why should that stop them from preaching doom and gloom?)

Well, we got tired of hearing all the naysayers in the world so we initiated a national business search to select a business owner we would work with for 120 days and *prove* it was possible to take a business to the next level in an incredibly short period of time. We combined the efforts with companies such as Dunn and Bradstreet, Hoovers, Comcast, and AllBusiness.com to promote our search, and we winnowed down the 1,000-plus applicants to 14 finalists. Their businesses were as diverse as a consulting business, manufacturing company, construction firm, collections agency, professional services firm, lifestyle company, and cruise line. In the end, we chose a small software company located in Arizona owned by Jennifer Lyle.

Jennifer had taken over the software company after buying out two partners a few years before our challenge began. At that time, the business had stagnated as the typical Middle Stage Level Two business that revolved around its owner. Jennifer was open, positive, and extremely committed to take her business to the next level—exactly the type of business owner with whom we love to work.

How would you like to have the Maui Advisors select you and your business to work hand-in-hand with for an intense period to take your business to the next level? Well, that's exactly what we did with Jennifer. We helped her map out her business growth strategy. We helped her re-tool her sales team and define her sales offer. We helped her create her hiring plan. We held her accountable for how she spent her time so she did the things that would make the biggest difference for her business in the shortest amount of time.

The results? They speak for themselves. Within six months, Jennifer's sales were up over 80 percent and her profitability had jumped an impressive 150 percent!

But alas, despite the stellar results of this challenge, the naysayers of the world will still say it can't be done. They'll give you all sorts of reasons why you can't do this or shouldn't do that. And if you listen to them, what results are you guaranteed to get? The exact same results you're getting right now. *Nothing will change unless you commit and take action to make them change.*

If you can tune out the naysayers, or better yet, transform their input into an incentive to prove them wrong and aggressively grow your business, you're destined to take your business to the next level faster than you could imagine.

Whenever we're working with a business owner, we're always working toward that magic day when she finally "gets it" that she can have her business and have her life outside of it. Yes, it's possible. When you build your business the right way, you get both the money and the freedom.

Case Study: Marichiel

Speaking of naysayers, if we're really being honest with ourselves we are usually our own biggest critic. That was true for one of our clients, Marichiel. She was the typical middle income employee, working as a real estate appraiser. One of her very close friends was a client of ours who went on to found and scale a wildly successful health business.

Marichiel watched her friend succeed but kept telling herself she couldn't do it. That was until she suffered a family tragedy that shook her world. In a miraculous way, Marichiel came out of the sadness stronger and committed to be an example for her young son. She took a leap of faith and started her own appraisal company.

It was hard work in the beginning, but Marichiel was determined to succeed. She connected with an upgraded peer group of business owners in the Maui community, listened to our coaching, and followed the Level Three Road Map. Eighteen months later, she was working less than five hours a week in her flourishing appraisal company and had even started a second business!

Marichiel is a great example of what is truly possible if you can face down your inner naysayer. Here's how she expressed herself in a letter she sent to us:

"Not only do I have what you taught me, but so do my children and future generations to come. I am creating a legacy because of you. Thank you for creating Maui Mastermind."

In the next chapter, we'll dive deep into the Level Three Road Map and lay out the entire lifecycle of your business from launch to exit. Plus you'll learn why your Level Three business will be worth 10 times its Level Two counterpart!

The Level Three
Road Map in Detail

L et's take another pass through the Level Three Road Map, going into deeper detail and breaking down Level Two into three distinct stages: Early, Middle, and Advanced. At each stage, your Level Two business will have different characteristics and specific needs. You'll find that understanding this more detailed view of the Level Three Road Map will get you locked on course and focused on the right outcomes for your specific Level and Stage. In the end, this will shave years off your journey to Level Three.

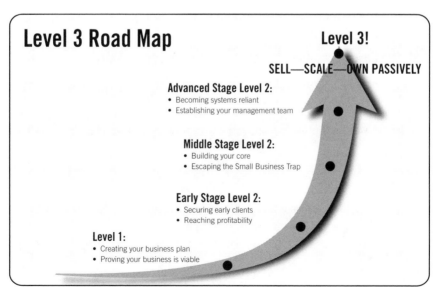

Level 3 Road Map

Level 3!

SELL—SCALE—OWN PASSIVELY

Advanced Stage Level 2:
• Becoming systems reliant
• Establishing your management team

Middle Stage Level 2:
• Building your core
• Escaping the Small Business Trap

Early Stage Level 2:
• Securing early clients
• Reaching profitability

Level 1:
• Creating your business plan
• Proving your business is viable

Level One: Planning Your Business and Proving It's Viable

At Level One, you're designing and planning your new start-up. You're gathering your initial team, raising any required start-up capital, and executing your launch plan. Your focus at Level One is to plan your new business and get immediate market feedback to learn if your business concept and model is economically viable. This is a fancy way to say you'll be testing your product or service to see if you can sell it at a price that allows your business to be profitable.

Take the example of Linda, a 20-year veteran of the medical sales field. Linda was a successful pharmaceutical and medical device sales representative with her MBA when we met her at a three-day workshop we hosted in San Diego.*

Tired of working for other companies, Linda wanted to build her own business helping small pharmaceutical companies and medical device manufacturers tap into an outsourced sales force of highly skilled and professionally managed sales reps to sell their pharmaceuticals or medical devices. On their own, these companies would never be able to afford this caliber of sales force.

Linda's choice for her business wasn't an accident. She applied a simple yet powerful formula that exponentially increased the chances of her new business succeeding. Looking closely at this formula, see if you can spot how Linda applied it. If you've already started a business, see if you intuitively followed this formula or if you strayed from it.

A Simple Formula to Know Which Business You Should Start

After observing thousands of our clients start businesses and seeing which ones thrived and which ones struggled, which succeeded and which failed, we've developed the following simple formula to help you know the business you should start. You'll find your highest likeli-

---

*For more detailed information on how you can attend one of these business owner workshops, go to **www.MauiMastermindBook.com**. This is a great way to meet other business owners who are also working to take their businesses to Level Three!

hood of success when your business falls within the overlap of three areas:

- Your passions
- Your talents
- Your advantages

Your Passions: What are you passionate about? What do you love to do? What things do you find absorbing? Engaging? Engrossing? To build a successful business requires focusing on your business long after the blush of the initial excitement has faded. Your passion keeps you in your business and enjoying it even when you're faced with the inevitable challenges.

For Linda, her passion was to help people—that is, she loved selling a product she believed in to people who could use that product to make a real difference in the lives of those they served.

Your Talents: What are you great at doing? What skills come easily and naturally for you? What do other people say looks easy when you do it? In what area are you consistently improving?

For Linda, her talents included a wonderful ease in meeting new people, the ability to build solid relationships, an infectious way of getting other people excited, and a dogged persistence that kept her focused on her goals, even when it looked like things might never work out.

Your Advantages: What are the resources, both financial and non-financial, that you can bring to your new business venture? What life experiences have you earned and want to apply? What relationships have you built that you can tap into? What skill sets and proficiencies have you invested the time and money to cultivate? What financial resources can you access? What symbolic capital have you earned?

In Linda's case, she spent 20 years in the medical sales arena. She had gained an intimate knowledge of how the industry worked, both from the standpoint of those selling in the field to the pharmaceutical or medical device companies that strive to make a profit. She had also developed relationships with hundreds of doctors, hospital administrators, medical staff members, sales reps, and medical companies. To all that, she brought a network of other business owners and advisors from the Maui community to give her feedback, help her fine-tune her plan, and support her in executing that plan.

The most successful start-ups live in the overlap of these three areas: your passions, your talents, and your advantages.

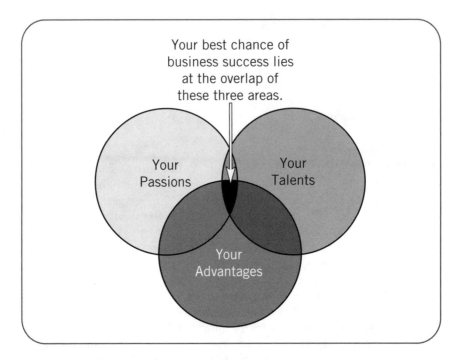

Before you decide which business to start, clearly list your passions, talents, and advantages. From there, look for a business opportunity that addresses the overlapping area of all three.

The 4 Action Steps You Must Take in Level One

Action Step 1: Clarify your basic business idea.

Let's say you've been dreaming of your new business for months or even years and playing the "what if" game in your head. It's time to get serious and turn your dreams into tangible, concrete ideas on paper. To clarify your core business concept, start by answering these seven questions:

1. In two or three sentences, describe your business idea.

2. Who is your ideal customer? Describe that person's characteristics in as much detail as possible.

3. What exactly will that ideal customer buy from you? Describe your product or service including the key features and benefits that will prompt your customers to buy it.

4. How much will your ideal customers pay? How and when will you collect that money?

5. Who will be your main competitors? List the most important ones.

6. What will separate you from your competitors? How will you find space in your market or niche to generate sales?

7. What is your dream for how you will expand and grow your business? What do you imagine it will look like in three to five years?

Action Step 2: Conduct your market research.

Before launching your business, invest the time and energy to do an intense period of market research. Study your prospective customers, your competitors, your likely key vendors, and your business advisors. Use this as a chance to sharpen your thinking, gather raw data, and record the information you'll need for your planning process. Get online and start Googling away. Phantom shop your competitors. Interview your prospective vendors. Talk with your advisors and mentors. See if you still want to move forward with your business idea. If you do, determine how you can refine it to increase your odds of success.

Action Step 3: Write your business plan "draft."

A business plan is the written outline for how you will launch your new business. Too many business owners never take time to write one because they find it intimidating. However, you don't need to create a *perfect* business plan; you just need to use it as a template. It will help you refine your thinking, organize your thoughts, and identify the questions you need to ask. You don't need to have all the answers, but you do need to identify the questions you must pay attention to—immediately and over time. Your business plan will help you create a clear action plan with defined next steps, timelines, and deliverables. In addition, if you need to raise outside capital, your business plan will be essential to helping you fund your new company.

Note how we suggest writing a "draft" of your business plan. We do this intentionally to reinforce the concept that your business plan *will always be a work in progress* and you don't have to get it perfect. It's the process of doing the plan and updating it annually that's so useful.

The graphic "Outline for Your Business Plan" shows a practical outline of what your business plan will include. Don't worry if this seems like a lot; you can find powerful tools and resources to help you create your business plan.*

---

*To simplify things for you, we've put together a comprehensive list of the books, workshops, and software tools we recommend you use to both create a business plan and launch your business more successfully. To access this list, go to **www.MauiMastermindBook.com**.

Remember, writing a "draft" gets you to start organizing your thinking and capturing the questions you'll need to answer as you launch and grow your business.

Outline for Your Business Plan

1. Executive Summary
2. Big Picture View
   a. Business you are trying to build (What do you want your business to look like in three to five years?)
   b. Exit strategy (What do you imagine you will want to do once you've built this successful business? Will you sell it? Scale it? Own it passively?)
   c. Mission, vision, values
   d. Business model you're using
   e. Big picture strategy
3. Marketing Plan
   a. Target market (who your ideal customers are and who they are not)
   b. Products and/or services (what your customers are buying from you, including details of your offer)
   c. Competitive analysis (who your potential competitors are and their strengths and weaknesses)
   d. Market trends
   e. Key marketing leverage points (where small investments of time and money will yield magnified returns)
   f. Marketing strategy (how you plan to reach your ideal customers)
   g. Marketing action plan (how you'll execute on your strategy with clear priorities, deliverables, and deadlines)
4. Sales Plan
   a. People (who will sell your products/services and how you'll compensate them)
   b. Process (what sales process and tactics you'll use to close business)

(continued)

    c. Lead management (how you'll organize and handle your leads)

    d. Collateral (what sales materials you'll need to develop at the start)

    e. Key sales leverage points (where small investments of time and money will yield magnified returns)

    f. Sales action plan (how you'll actually start selling)

5. Operational Plan

    a. Fulfillment (how you'll fulfill or deliver on your product/service)

    b. Admin/corporate (what infrastructure you'll need to put in place)

    c. Staffing needs/hiring plans/role description

    d. Operating budget (what it will cost to run your business)

    e. Cost factors (the biggest factors and how you plan to control them)

    f. Operational action plan with clear priorities and deliverables (who will do what by when and what criteria you'll use to measure success)

6. Management Team (most important if you need to use your business plan to raise outside capital)

    a. Members (who's on the leadership team and what roles they will fill)

    b. Expertise (what background, talents, experience sets, and other advantages your key team members will bring)

    c. Organizational chart (what it will look like in the beginning)

7. Financial Projections

    a. Current financials (if the business is already operating)

    b. Proforma projections (over the next 12-month and 36-month periods)

    c. Breakeven analysis (at what point revenues will equal expenses)

    d. Cash flow analysis (over the next 12-month period)

    e. Capital requirements to start (with details of how funds will be specifically used)

Author's Note: The subject of creating a business plan is so important that we've recorded a more detailed online workshop to help you create your plan effectively. To immediately access this FREE online workshop, simply go to **www.MauiMastermindBook.com**. See Appendix A for details.

> ### David's Story
>
> I drafted my first business plan about 13 years ago for a business I later sold for a multimillion-dollar payday. This business plan was only six pages! Looking back, I used very few of the stated ideas in the business that I ultimately grew. *But*—an awfully big *but*—the exercise of writing it and updating it two to three times a year helped keep me focused. It required me to stay clear on where my priorities and attention needed to be as I grew the business.

Action Step 4: Test your product or service to make sure it will sell.
If your new business involves selling a product or service that customers are already buying from someone else, then you just need to know you can attract enough new or existing customers to buy from *you* so that your business will succeed. But what if your product or service is new? Then you have to find a quick, fast, and cost-effective way to see if people actually *will* buy it before you go to the expense of investing time and money in large amounts. This might mean creating and selling a prototype. Or you might sell a service you have to establish as you go. Or you can canvass members of your target market and gauge their feedback on whether they would buy if it were available. In any case, use your best efforts to get objective feedback and test the waters on the viability of your business idea.

Tourists versus Locals

> ### David's Story
>
> I was walking in my neighborhood when down the street I noticed that a car had pulled up to a pedestrian to ask him for directions. As I got closer I overheard the pedestrian apologize and explain that he was from out of town and didn't know his way around. I politely stepped in and gave the family directions. Later that day I thought, "This is exactly the mistake many new business owners make when they ask friends and family for feedback on their new business idea."
>
> If you want market feedback about your business offering, ask the locals—the people or businesses in your target market. If you listen to every "tourist" in your life, you'll be getting directions from a visitor like that pedestrian who didn't know his way around at all!

Proving your idea is viable means determining if the market will buy your product or service *from you* at a price that can be profitable. What's the best guarantee of getting accurate information? Actually close a sale! You can sell a prototype and deliver later; you can sell someone else's product or service that you buy wholesale; you can even sell the product or service and just go back the next day and refund the money, explaining you have a delay in your ability to deliver. Yes, you may lose a sale, but at least you'll know you can actually *make* that sale! This confirmation is worth the world to you in Level One when you're wondering if you can sell your product or service at a profitable price for your business.

So what happens if your test marketing shows you can't get any sales? Does this mean your business won't work? Not necessarily. It just means your business won't fly in its current form. But before you redo your entire product or service, experiment with your sales and marketing efforts. Tweak those first. Not only are they the cheapest elements to change, but they're the most likely reason no one was buying.

If your offering still doesn't sell after improving the way you sell and market, then reexamine the product or service itself. How should you change it to make it sell?

Do you need to:

- simplify the product or service?
- add more features or more depth?
- change the timing of the product's delivery?
- tweak the way you package the product or service?
- bundle your offer with other products or services?
- consider other possibilities?

The goal of Level One is to plan your new business by drafting a business plan, then get direct market feedback to prove that it's viable. When you've accomplished this, it's time to move to Level Two Early Stage.

Level Two Early Stage:
Making Your Business Sustainable

Focus: Securing your early clients and becoming profitable.

Leverage Points: Your ability to change and adapt, keeping costs low and your business lean.

Fresh in the marketplace, an Early Stage Level Two business has just started actively marketing and selling its products/services. This is the time to learn your business and market, and if needed, discover and cure any fatal flaws in your business model or in the way your targeted customers perceive the value you're creating.

Your early focus while launching a business isn't on building the perfect product or service, but rather on figuring out how you can get people to buy. Too many entrepreneurs get caught in the trap of making the perfect gizmo, but never actually *sell that gizmo in large enough numbers* to ensure a profit.

Know that at this stage in your business's growth, you'll be wearing just about every hat in the business. That's okay for now, but as you move toward Middle Stage Level Two, you'll need to find ways to leverage your personal production for the business by hiring staff and building basic business systems.

Remember, an Early Stage Level Two business is working to generate sales, establish a market position, and become a sustainable business.

Priority #1: Sell, Sell, Sell!

Focus initially on your sales and marketing—it's critical! If you can't sell your product or service, you don't have a sustainable business. So pull out your business plan and start executing the marketing and sales plan you laid out in your business plan draft.

Create your "top prospect list" and start making sales calls. (Alternatively, if your marketing plan calls for selling via channel partners or joint venture partners, then get to work calling on them.)

Who are your top 25 prospective customers or joint venture/channel partners? Listing what you know about your top prospects helps you gather information that leads to those all-important early sales. So start a file on each of them and include the following information:

1. Why is this customer such a great client/partner lead?

2. Why is your business a great fit for what this customer needs?

3. Who do you know inside those organizations? Who could personally introduce you to these people or organizations, whether they're insiders or not?

4. Who are the decision makers? If you're selling directly to consumers, how, when, and where do they normally make their buying decisions on your product/service? How do you get in front of those decision makers?

Execute your marketing plan. This might call for you to:

- sell at a trade show or at local markets.
- rent direct mail lists of prospects to mail and call.
- network for leads at your local chamber of commerce and other groups.
- buy key word advertising to generate traffic to your website.
- actively post to discussion forums and blogs to spread the word about your business.
- use social media (Facebook, Twitter, LinkedIn, etc.) to get the word out.

At this juncture, it's essential that you secure an adequate lead flow so you not only generate the sales needed to become profitable, but you can also develop your base sales and marketing system.

To create a successful business requires more than just making a sale here or there. You've got to build it in a way that will reliably generate ongoing sales. You need this dependable stream of sales in order to build the baseline marketing and sales system that you can later scale.

Case Study: John

A short while ago, a business owner named John came to us with a difficult dilemma. His new teleconference company was an Early Stage Level Two business with sales that covered about 70 percent of its costs. He had an exciting opportunity to change the company's business model for the better. He had reached a crossroads and knew it. He wanted our input to help him make a pivotal decision between shifting focus to this new venture or staying with his original business model.

Too many business owners make poor and costly decisions simply because they're too close to their businesses and don't have the perspective they need to see things accurately. That's a huge benefit of having outside peers and advisors you can turn to in order to provide this perspective. That's also why we think it's difficult and dangerous to build your business in isolation.

First, we asked John objective questions so we could accurately view his situation and desired outcome, and then determine his realistic options. After going through our question sequence, three things became clear to John. First, his new business model was unproven and hence a gamble, but also one with a big upside if successful. In fact, if it worked, he would be creating a brand new market that his business could dominate. Second, his current business efforts were working; conservatively, they were five months away from becoming profitable. Third, once he reached profitability under his existing business plan, it would be fairly straightforward to maintain and incrementally grow the current sales volume.

Once these key data points were laid out, his decision became easy. John chose to aggressively focus on reaching profitability under his existing business plan. This would give him the financial strength and sustainability he needed to take a chance and refocus some of his best talent on establishing this new market and developing his new business model.

When faced with a tough business decision that has serious consequences, we suggest getting structured, outside input to help clarify the current situation, your desired outcome, and your potential options. This is when you lean on your peers and advisors to help you think through your situation and the best choices. It's too easy to get locked into a stunted perspective. Besides, building any business in isolation is expensive, painful, and inefficient. We all need peers and advisors in our lives—people we can turn to and trust with tough decisions.

Priority #2: Start Creating Simple Systems and Structure to Operate Your Business

Remember, you aren't building permanent systems yet; rather, you're building your initial rudimentary systems to help you generate leads, close sales, and fulfill on client purchases.

Stephanie's Story

When we originally took over Pacific Plastics and Engineering, the old owner had no formal business systems in place. We quickly learned that our customers were fed up with the

(continued)

Stephanie's Story (continued)

long history of broken promises that the old owner had made but not honored. One of the first things we did was visit each of the customers. We sat down and talked with them to learn what they felt our business had promised them. Needing a way to capture and organize those promises, we laid them all out in a spreadsheet. The spreadsheet listed orders, delivery dates, and pricing information. This was one of our earliest business systems. Later, we expanded our systems to include an actual production manual for each of our manufacturing orders.

Now, years later, we have a comprehensive and formal enterprise resource planning system that lays out each step in the process: quoting and pricing of new projects; automatic scheduling of incoming orders; engineering and machine setup; large-scale production; on-time delivery of all customer orders; and input into the financial system.

The system we use today took several years to develop and wasn't something we could have laid out at the start of our business. We didn't know enough; the business wasn't developed enough. It's an iterative process wherein you start with the best system you can create and over time refine and redesign all your systems continually.

So start where your business is today and build a few rough systems to guide your work. You'll get more consistent results with less time, effort, and expense. Later, you can expand and upgrade your systems, but don't wait to start creating systems until you have the time and expertise to get them all done. Add one system at a time as you can. Take the first step now!

You'll find plenty of time to develop articulated business systems later. For now, make sure your business can survive, which means selling and delivering on your promises to customers and clients. At first, this can be as simple as creating an order form for taking phone orders, composing a checklist for all the deliverables due to your clients, or setting up an auto-responder email that thanks all new customers for their online orders. Later, this might mean creating an online project management system for doing a trade show, setting up a company database (most likely hiring it out), or creating a work-flow process that details how you work with a new client.

You won't ever have time to sit down and write out all your business systems in one fell swoop. This is not only an unreasonable fantasy; it would actually be quite dangerous. Why? Two reasons. First, at this stage, you are needed to both generate sales and handle part, if not all, of the operational side of your business. If you stop all this to exclusively create systems, your business will die.

Think of it like your beating heart. Just as your body needs blood circulating, your business needs sales and cash flow. The key is to build your systems and infrastructure *while* maintaining your focus on generating sales and fulfilling your client promises.

Second, you don't yet have the experience to build out all your systems successfully. You have so much to learn from the practical experiences of growing your business. Regard building systems as an iterative process—one you simply do bit by bit.

David's Story

At our Business Owner Success Conferences, I'm often asked if someone can start a new business at Level Three. The answer is yes—*if* you buy a well-designed, successful Level Three business! Other than that, I'm afraid you'll have to do the work of growing your business through each successive level and stage.

However, once you've mastered the skill of building a Level Three business—or if you team up with peers and advisors who've already accomplished that—you can build it much faster than you'd think.

Priority #3: When Your Business Can Afford It, Begin to Build Your Team

In most cases, your early hires will be employees or outsourced service providers you can use to leverage your time as the key producer for your business. Building your team might include:

- hiring on more office staff,
- recruiting a part-time sales person, and/or
- outsourcing financial record keeping to a bookkeeper.

As you bring on new team members, take the opportunity to create the "system" for how to do each specific job. There won't be a better time than when you place a new person in the role. Then enlist each new hire in creating a rough system for how someone else in the role could best perform it.

Word of caution: Don't hire all at once. Rather, hire as you need to, making sure your business has the cash flow to afford the help.

Stephanie's Story

One of my biggest limitations early on in business was my struggle to hire the right people. Part of me wanted to rehabilitate and groom people for better and higher positions in the company. However, I've learned that you can't ascribe ambition to someone else. Some people are merely looking for a job and don't have the drive to build a career in which they're known for something special.

Looking back, I can see that many times I was too quick to hire and too slow to fire. I didn't take enough time getting to know job candidates to really understand if they wanted just a job or a career. And later when I did see that someone was the wrong fit, I didn't make the hard decision to let that person go fast enough. We need people who just want jobs and people who are looking to fulfill on their careers—I just had to figure out which were which!

Well, I sure learned my lesson. Today at my company, we have a comprehensive hiring process that includes three rounds of interviews and reference checks. Also, when we make a hiring mistake, we fix it right away. Remember, the right team will make a huge difference for your company, just as a bad hire will be a drag on your entire organization.

The goal of Early Stage Level Two is to create a sustainable business. When you've achieved this, then it's time to move to Level Two Middle Stage.

Level Two Middle Stage: Establishing Your Business Core

Focus: Establishing your business's foundation; building your business's core systems and structure

Key Leverage Point: Leveraging your time so you can invest at least 20 percent (one day a week) to building your business's core

Characteristics of a Typical Middle Stage Level Two Business:

- Business revolves around the owner.

- Owner must show up each day or the business suffers from the absence.

- Owner hits a revenue plateau; can't work any harder or put in any more hours.

- Outside world—especially customers—identify the business with only the owner.

Why do most businesses *never* make it past Middle Stage Level Two? Because the owners are entrenched in the traditional way of building a business for control and active cash flow based primarily on their personal production. Not only do they quickly max out on personal production, but what's worse is that every day, more and more of the know-how to run the business gets buried deeper in one person's head—instead of being captured in processes, procedures, and systems.

Sadly, these typical Middle Stage Level Two business owners stay stuck at the tactical level of doing the *job* the business requires instead of creating the time and space to step back and *build the business itself.*

Middle Stage Level Two requires building your core systems, controls, and scalable solutions. The challenge is doing that while balancing the business's need for you to continue to lead its daily operation. This is a delicate balance between what your business needs today and what it will need tomorrow. Thankfully, you don't have to figure all this out yourself.

The Level Three Road Map shows that, at Middle Stage Level Two, you have to build out the baseline systems for the following five areas:

1. **Your "Master System"—the system of all your systems.** This Master System involves how you organize, store, access, and update most of your business systems. It can be an operations manual, a grouping of files on a server, or a comprehensive enterprise software solution. (See Chapter 4.)

2. **Your "Core Systems."** This includes key systems to generate leads, close sales, fulfill on customer orders, and deliver on client promises.

3. **Your most pressing business controls, especially those around the financial area.** These include accounts receivable, accounts payable, and financial record keeping and reporting, all of which help you manage your cash flow and protect against financial

abuses. You also want to design your first rough dashboard showing how your business as a whole is performing at any given moment.

4. **Your big-picture strategic plan.** This includes your business priorities, plan of action, and branding and market positioning.

5. **Your initial team.** These are the early team members you'll lean on as you grow your business. You've still got to hire cautiously due to both cash flow concerns and your business's immaturity, but now is the time to begin hiring high order talent—slowly and deliberately. You'll also start systematizing the "Team" area of your business by developing written job descriptions, a draft organizational chart, and a formal hiring process.*

As you learned in the last chapter, the average small-business owner gets trapped at Middle Stage Level Two inside the Self-Employment Trap. But not you! Instead, you can follow the Level Three Road Map and use this stage as a launching pad to start scaling your business.

In essence, this means developing your core systems and controls, hiring and aligning your initial team, and clarifying your strategic plan to get you to Level Three.

Case Study: Lainy

Lainy was a finalist in our national business search mentioned earlier. She and her husband had built a highly successful heavy manufacturing business, but that business strictly revolved around the two of them. She ran the operations and financial areas of the business while her husband ran the sales and marketing end.

In a way, Lainy and her husband suffered from the curse of competency that hurts many capable entrepreneurs. They were smart, driven, and incredibly talented at doing the work of the business. They also were particular about how they wanted things to be done. This combination of factors lured them into building their business for control, which you already know leads to the Self-Employment Trap.

But when you have the right road map to follow and the strong, clear commitment to scale your business as Lainy did,

---

*Would you like to watch a 30-minute video clip from our Business Owners Success Conference where we share our 5-step hiring process? Just go to **www.MauiMastermindBook.com**. See Appendix A for details.

things can shift quickly. Within nine months of joining our consulting program, Lainy's business had jumped to Advanced Stage Level Two. She had implemented systems that got her out of much of the day-to-day operations. She had hired her first executive leader, a CFO, to run the financial side of the business and provide a balanced "voice" to help her and her husband make better leadership decisions. Her sales were up and the company was in the process of expanding to a second manufacturing facility. Her discretionary time had increased by more than 15 hours a week, allowing her to reinvest this time in expanding the business.

All this in fewer than nine months!

You see, it doesn't take decades to build a Level Three business, but it does take both a clear commitment to get there and a concrete road map to follow. In Lainy's case, she always had the commitment; she just didn't have the road map before getting involved in the program.

As a Middle Stage Level Two business, you're scrambling to do two things: (1) bring organization to the chaotic world of your new business, and (2) impose this order in a way that enhances your sales.

Once you build out your core as described in Middle Stage Level Two, you'll progress to Advanced Stage Level Two and begin the important work of refining your systems, building your management team, and scaling your business in earnest.

Level Two Advanced Stage: Building a Systems-Reliant Company with a Winning Management Team

Focus: Increasing your capacity and scaling your business

Key Leverage Point: Your key team members' time, talent, skills, and focus

Characteristics of a Typical Advanced Stage Level Two Business: As you begin to transition into Advanced Stage Level Two, your business will commonly have the following characteristics, which become your starting point:

- It's becoming more and more systems driven. (At least one or two of the five main areas of your business are managed by people other than you.)

- Your revenue is starting to climb.
- Your business may feel like it's bursting at the seams.

The Level Three Shift

An essential piece in building a Level Three business is enrolling your team in building the systems, controls, and scalable solutions with you. Rather than regarding the team around you as a form of leverage that magnifies your personal reach and production, instead see them as partners in taking the business to the next level. As management guru Peter Drucker once said, *"The founder has to learn to become the leader of a team rather than a 'star' with 'helpers.'"*

David's Story

While I understand how to read and use financial statements, I don't know how to prepare them or keep them updated. And for sure I'm the wrong person to build out the financial controls needed in a business. In our company, Susan, our CFO, set up our financial systems and controls. As a CPA, she has the experience, skill set, and interest to build out the financial area of our Maui Mastermind business. Before she made that her focus, the area was a mess. But within 12 months of taking on the job, Susan had put formal procedures and working systems in place that strengthened the business.

Remember, the right team members want to build the parts of the business they're best at creating. You simply need to hire wisely and then get out of their way so they can get the job done.

Stephanie's Advice

Too many business owners are afraid of hiring better, smarter, more experienced team members to lead areas of their business, as if the presence of these team members threatens to eclipse the insecure owner. I've always believed in hiring top people and giving them the resources and support to do a world-class job. In fact, this has been the single biggest secret that Jack and I have discovered on our journey to Level Three.

Building a Winning Management Team

Reaching Level Three requires finding and enlisting key members to "own" parts of your business. More important, it requires you to let go of control so your business can thrive without you.

Rather than have all roads lead back to and through you like a hub in the middle of a wheel, encourage your team to work with each other directly. Grow their capacity to make their own decisions and take the initiative within the company. Remember, a business dependent on its owner—you—for its success becomes a prison that traps you. Plan for your great prison escape *now* by building your management team. Before long, you'll have key leaders in each of the five core pillars of your business: sales/marketing, operations, team, finance, and executive leadership. (See Chapter 4 for more details.)

In addition, make sure that your leaders and team members have a unified vision of what the business is, where it's heading, and how you plan to get there. This lets you set clear priorities, assign responsibilities, and hold each other accountable for results.

Criteria that Determine When You've Reached Level Three

What exactly does it look like when you've reached Level Three? First, you'll have solid leaders in place in four of the five core areas of your business. Yes, you may still hold on to the role of CEO for a while, provided you still enjoy a daily involvement leading the business. But you have the strategy, systems, and traditions in place to hire a new CEO if you choose. That means your business would thrive even if you were only there two or three days a month. (Think Chairman of the Board.)

This signifies that your business is so strong, its success is independent of any single team member, including you, the owner. Also, it has clear processes and procedures to run all five areas: sales/marketing, operations, team, finance, and leadership. You have an enterprise-level dashboard that allows you and your team to know the status and health of your business at any given moment. Finally, you have the clear traditions and culture to help keep your business true to its vision, mission, and values even after you aren't present every day.

Since you've built out your systems and developed your management team, you're now ready to take that last step to Level Three.

Level Three: Owning a Business That Gives You Freedom and Control

Focus: To determine your desired exit strategy and clarify your personal role

Characteristics of a Typical Level Three Business:

- The business is run by a competent and winning management team independent of the owner (who may still fill one of the roles, but who has a replacement groomed and ready to step in).
- The business runs smoothly whether the owner is there or not over an extended period of time (based on sound systems, intelligent controls, and scalable solutions).
- Its clients look to the business, not the owner, to fulfill promises.

The 3 Exit Strategies for You and Your Level Three Business

Every story needs a great ending or you're left feeling dissatisfied. Your business story needs a great ending, too. We call this your exit strategy.

As you'll learn, this may or may not mean actually selling your business. In fact, many Level Three business owners choose to stay actively engaged. What's the critical distinction? Continued involvement is a personal *choice*, not a business *requirement*. That's right. You get to make that decision and choose any of these three main exit strategies:

1. You can sell the business and move on to your next great adventure.
2. You can scale the business to the big time.
3. You can passively own the business, with a greatly diminished role for yourself in its daily operation.

Let's go deeper into each of these three exit strategies so you get a sense of the end toward which you're working.

Exit Strategy 1: Sell

Once you've built a Level Three business, you've created a valuable asset with clear market value. Your first exit strategy is to harvest the equity you've built by selling the business.

Case Study: Jeff

After college, Jeff worked for a few years in corporate America. One day, his manager sat him down and told him he'd never be successful in business because he was impatient, lacked focus, and didn't follow the rules. This weighed heavily on Jeff, coming as it did from an authority figure—until months later, he had lunch with his mentor who had built several successful companies. This mentor said he knew Jeff would be a success because he had the natural drive to get things done now, the ability to multi-task, and a willingness to blaze new trails. *Same Jeff, different perspective.* Luckily, Jeff chose to listen to his multimillionaire mentor instead of his mid-level manager at work!

Knowing he wouldn't be satisfied working in corporate America, Jeff started his first software company, CTI, and grew it into a thriving innovator in the travel industry. He strategically positioned the company to be bought out by one of the industry's major players, which is exactly what happened. American Express acquired CTI for more than $10 million!

Since that time, Jeff has gone on to build and later sell other successful companies.

5 Types of Buyers for Your Level Three Business

When you sell a Level Two business, generally the only interested buyers are mom-and-pop entrepreneurs who want to buy a job for themselves. It's when you reach Advanced Stage Level Two and Level Three that you appeal to a wider pool of potential buyers.

Here are the five main types of buyers for your Level Three business:

1. **Strategic Buyers:** Strategic buyers look at your business and want to buy it as an operating entity. They want to maximize its value to them after buying it. Usually, this means they want to integrate the business into their existing business frame. This might mean buying your business for assets such as a patent or other technology or trade secrets, for the value of its brand, or for your customer list and relationships.

A strategic buyer could be a competitor, a key customer, or a large vendor, or it could be a new entrant looking to buy into an advantageous position in your industry.

Generally, you'll get the highest price from strategic buyers because they have the opportunity to reduce overhead after the sale by consolidating your business into theirs. They also tend to have the best knowledge and experience to maximize your business afterward, plus they have a high comfort level with your industry, product line, and customer relationships.

2. **Private Equity Buyers:** Private equity buyers are looking at your business as a financial investment with their eyes squarely on "ROI" (Return on Investment). These private equity companies are generally only interested in buying if they can see a clear way to get out of the investment profitably within a three- to five-year time horizon. Remember the case study of Morgan in Chapter 2? This situation involved a sale to a private equity firm. The company that bought Morgan's company did what's called an "industry roll up." This is when an investment group acquires several small- to medium-sized companies in a target industry. They intend to integrate these acquisitions into a larger whole that will be worth more because it has acquired a certain scale.

3. **MBO—Management Buy Out:** This is when the top managers in your company team up to buy you out. Typically, they put up a portion of the purchase price themselves and then find outside investors or financing to cover the remainder of the purchase price. This type of sale tends to be less disruptive to your employees because the management team in place remains essentially the same after the sale.

4. **ESOP—Employee Stock Ownership Program:** This is a special type of sale of the business to its employees. Strong tax incentives support this type, but generally you'd receive the lowest price of all the options if you choose this one.

5. **Going Public:** One final way to sell your business is to sell it to the public through a public stock offering. For example, former Maui Advisor Jeff Hoffman helped found Priceline.com in 1997. He was part of the team that launched the company and eventually took it public two years later in March of 1999. Currently, Priceline.com has a market value (called its Market Cap) of over *$9 billion*!

3 Steps to Take Today to Sell for Top Dollar Tomorrow

Stephanie's Story

Jack and I have known for years that one day we would sell our company. Our two kids don't have an interest in running it, and we've got a large amount of equity that we've built up over the years as we took the business to Level Three. We knew that selling it would be our way of harvesting that equity.

So several years back, we sat down with our CPA and talked with him about our future plans. He gave us one of the best pieces of concrete advice we've ever gotten. He said to plan for the eventual sale years *in advance* instead of down the road. He gave us a long document that listed out all the things that buyers would require us to show them as part of their due diligence. The list included audited financials, employee records, corporate minutes, and on and on. Some people might find that list intimidating and just let it fall away, but smart business owners know that by preparing two to three years in advance to sell their companies, they will command higher valuations and have an easier time finding the right buyer down the road.

The most important question you can ask yourself is this: *"What can I do today to prepare to sell my business two to three years from now?"* Here are three concrete steps to follow as you prepare now to sell later.

Step 1: Determine what your business is currently worth.
How do you find out what your business is currently worth? You can look to industry or association sources for the most common valuation methods for your type of business. You can hire a valuation firm, work with an investment banker, or even hire a CPA experienced in your industry and type of business. Even more important is understanding how companies in your industry and business category are valued by the market. What formula is most commonly used? What is the current range of business multipliers and how can you command the top end of that range? Find out!

Step 2: Do a "buyer's audit."
Put yourself in the shoes of a potential buyer and take a hard, long look at your business. Which elements give it value in an outsider's eyes? What major risks do you see that scare you? What are the most attractive parts

of buying this specific business versus one of its competitors? What are the least attractive parts of buying it? If you could change only three things to make it more attractive as an acquisition, what three specific things would you change over the coming 12 months?

The 6 Key Risks from a Buyer's Perspective

1. **Management team:** How talented are the managers? Will they stay? What happens if one or more leave? Who will lead the enterprise as a whole?

2. **Reliance on owner:** Will this business work well without you (the owner) around? Which customers rely on your personal relationship to keep them happy? What banking relationships are based on your personal financials or rapport with a specific banker?

3. **Truth and accuracy of financial records:** Are your financial records clean and up to date? Have your financials been audited by outside firms? Are there any warning flags like discrepancies between corporate tax returns, filings, or investor reporting and the company financials?

4. **Customer base (concentration and future prospects):** Are the customer relationships with the company or with the owner? Is any one customer so big that the business would suffer if that customer's orders diminished or went away altogether? What are the future prospects for your key customers? Your industry? Your specific business?

5. **Competition:** Where does your company stand in the marketplace compared to your competitors? How will you assure your prospective buyer that sales and market share can grow, not just be maintained?

6. **Industry future:** What trends affect your industry? What potential disruptors could kill your industry overnight? What contingencies do you have for these scenarios?

The bottom-line question is this: *"Are you taking action to mitigate as many perceived buyer risks as possible over the next two to three years before you sell?"**

---

*Would you like to watch a 50-minute video of Stephanie and David walking you through the key steps to selling your company? Then go to **www.MauiMastermind Book.com**. You'll get *instant* access to this advanced business owner training. See Appendix A for details.

Step 3: Mitigate risks and enhance value.
Once you've identified key risks (see 6 Key Risks on the previous page) and specific elements that create value, take preemptive action to lessen the buyer's risks and enhance your business's value. The more you mitigate risks and enhance value in the eyes of a future buyer, the more your company will be worth when you sell it.

Mitigating risks is half the equation; the other half is enhancing value. What can you do over the next few years to enhance your business's value? Can you grow your sales? Improve your margins? Develop protected intellectual property? More firmly establish a brand? Deepen competitive advantages? Build company systems? Grow the management team? List your action steps and do them!

Exit Strategy 2: Scale
We've addressed the concept of scaling throughout the book. In the context of exiting, scaling means that you, the business owner, firmly decide to stay actively involved in the business and grow it magnitudes bigger.

It may seem strange to call scaling an exit strategy, but many entrepreneurs who've built a Level Three business don't want to leave or sell it. Rather, they want to grow it to the next level, which we call scaling your business. This means you take a $15 million company and grow it to $150 million or $1.5 billion. This option gives you the greatest financial reward, but it also requires your continued commitment, often over five or ten years or even longer after your business has reached Level Three.

Case Study: Wayne

Wayne, a client of ours for about a year, partnered with two others to build a nuclear medicine testing laboratory chain. Together, they have scaled their company to its current $200 million size. Wayne and his partners still work full time in the business, driving its growth higher and higher. Building a billion-dollar business is well within their reach. It's an active road for them to follow, and they are choosing the exit strategy of scaling with their eyes wide open.

Exit Strategy 3: Own Passively
Once you've taken your business to Level Three, you can transition to a more passive role—owning the company without running it every day. If

you choose this exit strategy, you'll enjoy the ongoing cash flow from the business without regularly coming into the office. You'll still have responsibilities, but from an *owner's* viewpoint, not a CEO's or a manager's viewpoint.

To keep on top of things, we suggest regularly reviewing key scorecards and financials, and keep in contact with your management team every month. Most Level Three business owners we know (including ourselves) spend between five and 25 hours a month managing their business interests when things run smoothly. In the event they aren't performing well, taking a more active role may be necessary.

Stephanie's Story

We built Pacific Plastics so we'd have our "Week at a Glance" dashboard of key enterprise metrics that tell the story of the business. That means Jack and I can log into the system from anywhere in the world and see real-time numbers about how our business is performing. This gives us peace of mind knowing that our team is doing great things.

For me, the biggest adjustment to stepping out of the day-to-day activities has been experiencing a mental and emotional shift in my roles. Part of me wants to step in and solve problems, but I know doing that weakens the team. So I have to let those involved find their own way through the situations that come up. As an example, one of our key customers recently promoted a new quality manager. That person arbitrarily changed our company's quality standards on their orders without consulting with our people in advance. I sat on my hands and let my team handle it, which they did in an excellent fashion.

Remember that you'll have to make emotional and mental adjustments when you become a passive owner. Obviously, if I saw something that might jeopardize the company's health, I'd step up my involvement. It's my business after all. But barring that, I've got to let my leaders lead; otherwise, they'll feel frustrated and move on to other opportunities.

A Short Quiz to Determine Where You Are on the Level Three Road Map*

Now that we've gone through the complete lifecycle of your business from Level One to Level Three, what level and stage is your business in right now? Circle the statement below that presently best describes your business:

Level One: You're still working on your business plan, raising your start-up funding, and preparing to launch your new business.

Early Stage Level Two: Your business is in its infancy, scrambling to make those early sales and fulfill customer promises.

Middle Stage Level Two: Your business is sustainable. It works, but only if you're present to work for it. You're the main producer and director around whom your company revolves.

Advanced Stage Level Two: Your business is growing fast with leaders in two or more of your five core pillars. You're in the process of refining your business systems and building your management team.

Level Three: Your business is firing on all cylinders with leaders in at least four of your five core pillars. Your business is systems-reliant and ready for you to choose your exit strategy—to sell, scale, or own passively.

---

*For a more comprehensive assessment of exactly where your business stands on the Level Three Road Map, go to **www.MauiMastermindBook.com** and take the "Road Map Quiz." In less than three minutes you'll *know* where your business is starting from and be able to access free training videos designed for your specific Stage and Level.

A Little-Known Formula at the Heart of 325 of the Forbes 400

Before leaving this chapter, let's talk about how taking your business to Level Three impacts the *value* of your business.

Have you ever wondered how the wealthiest people in the world originally built their fortunes? If you analyzed the Forbes 400 list of richest people in the United States, you'd find that more than 325 of them got on the list by applying a simple formula (or being the heir of someone who applied this formula!). What is this formula? It's called a "business multiplier," and it's one of the greatest wealth leverage points of all time.

Let's explore the business multiplier concept by walking through the value of a fictitious business we'll call Maui, Inc. as it progresses through the Level Three Road Map.

Level One: Business Start-Up
Value: Zero

You probably already know that a business start-up is nothing more than an idea and a plan; as such, it has no value in the market. The only exception to this might be if the plan has intellectual property attached to it such as a patent that will be applied or a trade secret process that will be leveraged. So at Level One, the business value of our imaginary business, Maui, Inc., is *zero*.

Early Stage Level Two: Business Scrambling for Its Survival
Value: Very Little

At Early Stage Level Two, this business has few paying customers. It's desperately trying to secure more clients and fulfill its promises to them long enough to establish a secure base for the business.

At this stage, Maui, Inc. still has no real value other than that of its tangible assets, including its equipment, inventory, and fixtures (and even those won't be valued at more than a fraction of original cost), or some deeply discounted value of its current annual sales.

Middle Stage Level Two: A Successful Business that Revolves Around the Owner

Gross Sales:	**$500,000**
Net Profit:	**$150,000**
Value:	**$150,000**

Once Maui, Inc. has a consistent track record of generating profits, it gains value. But that value will be limited because the business depends on the owner being present and involved.

While every business has different valuation formulas, most Middle Stage Level Two businesses end up valued in the $50,000 to $500,000 range. The actual value will depend on the industry, the length of operating history, the value of its hard assets (e.g., inventory, equipment, etc.), and the sales volume of the business. But the biggest limitation to selling a Middle Stage Level Two business is its limited pool of buyers. Usually only mom-and-pop buyers will step into the owner's shoes and "own" their own jobs.

With Maui, Inc., let's make these two assumptions: (1) It's a service business with a profit margin of 30 percent, meaning 30 cents out of every dollar of sales ends up as net profit. (2) Its gross sales are $500,000, which means the business nets $150,000 per year.

So in this hypothetical example, we're pegging the value of Maui, Inc. at $150,000, which is one times its annual net income.

Advanced Stage Level Two: A Successful Business Much Less Reliant on the Owner's Presence to Function

Gross Sales:	**$3.4 million**
Net Profit:	**$1 million**
Value:	**$3 million**

Once Maui, Inc. hits Advanced Stage Level Two, it has key leaders employed in three of its core pillars. The business still benefits from the owner's leadership, but the company is becoming more systems-reliant every day. Sales are climbing fast. In fact, gross sales are $3.4 million dollars and net profit is $1 million per year.

While that $1 million profit sure feels good, even better is being an Advanced Stage Level Two business. At this stage, Maui, Inc. is now valued by a special formula called a business multiplier. The company is now valued at a multiple of its net profit, which is a simplification but an accurate one. Every industry has its own range of business multipliers used in valuing a business in that industry.

Here's the best part. As you progress to Level Three, not only is your business more valuable because you're increasing both gross sales and net profits, but you're also increasing the business multiplier that your business can command. For example, your business at Advanced Stage Level Two might only command a three or four times (3–4x) multiplier, but when you hit Level Three, you might command an eight or ten times (8–10x) multiplier.

In our example, at Advanced Stage Level Two we valued Maui, Inc. at three times (3x) its net profit, or $3 million. Let's see what happens when Maui, Inc. reaches Level Three.

Level Three: A Systems-Reliant Business with Winning Management Team in Place

Gross Sales:	**$10 million**
Net Profit:	**$3 million**
Value:	**$21 million**

By this point, your Level Three business operates like a well-oiled machine. Your winning management team is in place, and your business controls and systems allow you to scale the business.

In our example, Maui, Inc. has grown its gross sales to $10 million, providing $3 million per year of net profit. As a Level Three business, Maui, Inc. now commands a seven times (7x) business multiplier, pegging its value at seven times (7x) its net earnings, or $21 million!

Notice that sales at Maui, Inc. have grown by only 300 percent from when the business was an Advanced Stage Level Two business, but it's now worth seven times more. This demonstrates the multiplying power of leveraging a higher business multiplier!

Case Study: Jennifer

Let's return to Jennifer, the winner of our national business search, to see the impact of the work we did on the *value* of her business. When we started working together, she owned a Middle Stage Level Two business with annual sales of $1.2 million. Twelve months later, she had not only increased her sales to $2 million, but in the process, she had grown her business to Advanced Stage Level Two. Let's look at how this maturation of her business radically increased its value.

As a Middle Stage Level Two business, the pool of potential buyers for Jennifer's company was much smaller. That means fewer people want and can afford to pay for the business. Assuming she could get two times (2x) net earnings for her business at that stage (a realistic amount for this type of business at Middle Stage Level Two), the boost in sales by itself increased the value of her business from $750,000 to $1.5 million.

But she didn't only increase sales and profits. Jennifer took her business to Advanced Stage Level Two, reduced its reliance on her, created more durable systems, and began to scale her company. This likely doubled her business multiplier from two times (2x) net earnings to four times (4x) net earnings. This meant that 12 months after she won the contest, her company was worth $3 million. Think about it. Her $800,000 increase in sales along with maturing the business to Advanced Stage Level Two added *$2 million of enterprise equity!* How else can you earn $2 million in 12 months starting with an asset like hers?

But Jennifer's story doesn't finish there. Let's look forward 36–48 months when the company becomes a true Level Three business netting $3 million per year (the trajectory she is currently on). What will her business be worth then? Using the current four times (4x) net business multiplier, her business will be worth $12 million. But here's the exciting part. At Level Three, her business multiplier will increase most likely (for her industry) to six to eight times (6–8x) net earnings. This will give her an enterprise value of $18 to $24 million!

Imagine this were your business. Those years of hard work paid off, giving you these choices:

- Sell your business for $18 to $24 million.

- Own it passively and enjoy $3 million per year net profit.

- Stay actively engaged and scale the company into the big leagues, growing it to $100 million or more.

Combined with the increased sales and profits, this is how the business multiplier for your scalable Level Three business can quickly grow your net worth. And this is why 85 percent of the Forbes 400's wealth originally came from building Level Three businesses.

In the next chapter, we go deeper into the five core pillars that will support your Level Three business.

CHAPTER 4

The 5 Functional Pillars of Every Business

very business has five functional areas that carry the load and provide a stable base to support additional growth; that's why we call
them pillars. The five pillars are:

1. **Sales and marketing**—Responsible for defining your market,
   finding prospective customers, and generating sales.

2. **Operations**—Fulfills the promises the sales department makes,
   plus handles back-office functions.

3. **Human Resources, or Team**—Responsible for hiring, training,
   and reviewing your staff. It also makes sure you comply with local,
   state, and federal labor laws.

4. **Finance**—Deals with the accounting, manages your cash flow, and
   pays your bills.

5. **Leadership**—Responsible for the big-picture vision and strategy
   of your business. Leadership sets the direction, establishes priorities, and coordinates all efforts and resources affecting the other
   four pillars.

Let's look at each of these five pillars in detail. Remember, while your
business may not have formally separated its activities into these divi-
sions, it absolutely carries out each of these five functions because every
business must. So as you read this section, look for ways you can apply
various concepts, strategies, and tactics to upgrade your base and handle
additional growth so you can expand and scale your business.

Pillar 1: Sales and Marketing

No leads, no sales. No sales, no business. It's that simple.

Marketing is everything you do to get one of your offers in front of the right prospective buyers under the best conditions possible. Marketing crafts your company's identity and positions it in the hearts and minds of your marketplace so you consistently generate the volume of sales leads you need. You want leads that are primed and ready for your selling systems to convert into thrilled clients or re-purchasers.

Sales is everything you do to make your offers as effective as possible and to close selling opportunities. Your offers can be delivered in a variety of ways—from trained sales reps to a call center taking phone calls to a sales letter or print ad to an interactive website to a tradeshow team to a retail location. Remember, the Sales and Marketing Pillar finds clients, makes sales, and generates revenue; it's the part of your business that makes it rain cash.

Too many entrepreneurs only focus on this pillar because they *have* to, not because they *want* to. They feel intimidated by the idea of selling. But understand this: in Early and Middle Stage Level Two, it's crucial for you as the company founder to focus a majority of your energy on generating profitable sales. If you don't, your new business won't survive, let alone thrive. Only as you grow your business can you replace yourself from the functions of this pillar. Achieving that requires creating a profitable selling *system*.

In the early days of your business, you focus on making sure sales happen, which means meeting with clients and closing deals yourself. Later, however, you must shift your focus to creating repeatable and scalable selling systems that don't depend on your involvement.

For example, imagine you have a new software start-up. As the company founder, your early efforts will involve landing key joint venture relationships with established players in your industry so you can market through their existing client base and split the revenue generated. As your software company grows, you no longer meet with new joint venture partners. Instead, you focus on finding and hiring the talent to do that. Later, you'll ensure your business is developing systems that will consistently find and hire new sales talent for your team.

Or imagine you have a contracting business. Early on, you meet with prospective clients to give estimates and close sales. But this is a Level Two solution. To create a Level Three business, you need to build the *system* that generates those sales. This might mean creating advertising systems to generate leads, hiring and training new estimators to close business, and eventually hiring a sales and marketing manager to take over this pillar of your contracting business.

Setting Up Systems

Do you get the importance of setting up selling systems to build a Level Three business? They include the following components:

- **Lead generation** systems to consistently generate the lead volume needed to generate sales.
- **Lead conversion** systems to consistently convert leads into thrilled clients.
- **Tracking and reporting** systems to reliably measure the effectiveness of your marketing and sales efforts, allowing you to optimize your selling systems over time.

Because many sales systems employ live sales agents to close sales, your system might also need to include the processes you use to find, hire, and train new sales agents. Add to that the sales management processes you develop to lead, motivate, and grow your sales team over time. None of this is easy, but its rewards are huge.

David's Story

One of the companies I built originally was dependent on my partner and me to produce all the sales—and sell we did. The two of us generated several million dollars of sales each year. But it required long hours and even worse (from my perspective), lots of travel. In those days, I had to spend 10 days out of every month on the road selling and closing new business. Although I was making a lot of money, this sure wasn't the dream I had for myself.

Then we finally got smart and began building a sales team and systems that didn't need us to close sales. We built up our online sales to half a million dollars a year. We built a network of independent sales reps who sold another two to three million a year. And we created a whole new selling channel with joint venture partners that generated several million dollars of annual sales (split 50-50 with our joint venture partner).

All told, it took us 36 months to build and optimize these selling systems. In the process, we tripled our company's sales volume while radically reducing the dependence on me and my partner to generate sales. Best of all, I cut my travel time by 70 percent!

8 Sales and Marketing Questions Every Business Owner Must Ask

1. **What are your most effective systems for generating new leads for your business?** For example, referral relationships; online advertising; affiliate program; social media; display advertisements in industry journals; trade shows; etc.

2. **How could you scale up the best of these systems to bring in more business?** For example, establish clear tracking to ensure you know which leads are the right leads; scale up your ad buys or send out more marketing pieces; optimize your website for better search engine results; spend more on winning key word advertising campaigns; create formalized referral programs; etc.

3. **How can you make these systems more consistent, reliable, or dependable?** For example, create a master marketing calendar with clear dates and assigned deliverables; establish a proven control ad or direct mail letter; have a sales website used by your prospective customers who come to shop or gather information; establish clear metrics that allow you to know objectively what is and isn't working; etc.

4. **What are your least effective lead generation systems?** This is the best place to look when searching for ways to grow your business. Too many business owners try to fix or improve their bottom 20–40 percent. They'd be better off cutting these losing efforts and immediately reinvesting the saved time and money into scaling the top 20 percent of their lead generators.

5. **What are your most effective systems for closing sales?** For example, live sales people; direct mail letters; sales landing web pages; sales DVD; etc.

6. **How could you scale up the best of these systems or better use them with the leads you already have?** For example, hire more sales reps; invest in technology to better handle the lead flow you currently have; create an automated follow-up selling system; design a website to effectively sell; move from selling one-to-one to one-to-many by hosting online webinars or live events; etc.

7. **How can you make these systems more consistent, reliable, or dependable?** For example, draft a best sales script; create a PowerPoint template all your sales team use to make their sales presentations; etc.

8. **What are your least effective sales conversion systems?** Again, this is the place to make immediate improvements to your sales in the shortest period of time. Rather than "fix" them, scrap your losing systems and leverage the selling systems that are working best. At the very least, take the elements of your winning sales systems (e.g., scripting, offer, pricing, sales logic, etc.) and incorporate them in your worst performers.

Scale Your Winners and Starve Your Losers

With the possible exception of your Finance Pillar, in no other area of your business is it as important to track your results as in sales and marketing. Do that by creating simple scorecards that tell you what *is* and *is not* working.

Do you know quantitatively and objectively how each of your main lead generation activities perform? For example, do you know your cost-per-lead by lead source? Do you know your percentage response rates (e.g., click-through rates on banner ads, or response rates per direct mail piece, etc.)? Are you able to relate your lead generation activities to your sales conversion metrics so you can track which leads are highest (or lowest) quality?

After you have good numerical data with which to work, determine your best lead generators, your best lead converters, and your best current client resellers, and invest in scaling up those efforts. How do you get the resources to do this? Easy. Starve your losers! Cut your bottom performers. Don't waste precious time, focus, and money on below-average performers when you can reinvest these resources in scaling up the best ones.

12 Powerful Techniques to Rapidly Increase Your Sales

To end this section on your Sales/Marketing Pillar, we wanted to give you these 12 additional techniques to immediately boost your sales and increase your cash flow.

1. **Reactivation offer:** Every business has customers and clients who used to buy but stopped for one reason or another. Many of these customers would buy again if you reached out and asked them to come back. Create a formalized selling system wherein, on a semi-annual basis, you gather your best past customers and make them an enticing offer.

David's Story

We used the reactivation offer technique with Maui Mastermind participants and generated more than $15,000 of sales with one email, not to mention tens of thousands of additional sales because we reestablished relationships with these quality clients. Our past clients not only got a great offer, but those who said yes felt great about being invited back to actively participate in the Maui community of business owners.

Too many businesses don't reach out to past clients because they're afraid of what they might discover. I believe that not only will most of your past clients feel grateful that you reached out, but the ones who don't will have valuable feedback you can use to improve your business.

2. **Makeup offer:** This calls for leveraging a customer complaint or cancelled order into a prime opportunity to simultaneously make a new sale and deepen a client relationship. For example, imagine Sarah emails your office that the widget she bought from you didn't work well. You have a systematized response that first auto-responds saying you received her email and one of your customer care team members will follow up within the next 48 hours. When your customer care agent follows up, either by email or phone, he not only listens to the problem Sarah experienced, probing to better understand the situation and gathering data to improve the company, but he also offers Sarah a special "thank you" gift for caring enough to tell you about the problem. This gift—like a $50 gift certificate for any of your products or 30 percent off her next order—should prompt Sarah to buy again. In the process, Sarah feels validated and respected, and you deepen a client relationship, learn something about your business, and spark another sale. Everybody wins.

3. **Upsell:** An upsell is an upgraded offer to customers that prompts a percentage of them to buy a more expensive package or item from your business. For example, if you run a home repair business and someone pays you to repair something, after you fix it, you could upsell them on a home warranty plan. *The best time to offer a client something better to buy is immediately at the point of purchase.* How could you upsell your customers to a higher value, richer product or service from your company?

4. **Cross sell:** Perhaps you don't have an upgraded package to sell your clients. What else do you have that they need and can purchase from you? For example, if you have a travel agency and you book a customer's airline tickets, see if you could also make the hotel booking or reserve a rental car.

5. **Rejection sales:** Every business has prospective clients who said no. What does your company do with these rejections? Most businesses never do anything with them. We urge you to not only build in strong follow-up systems, but also consider other ways to profit from these leads. Perhaps you could turn them over to a special sales team inside your business. Or you could sell these leads to another business. Or you could make them a "godfather" offer—one that's too good to refuse! Or . . . you get our point. You've already invested money to generate these leads; it's up to you to creatively market to them.

6. **Stale leads:** These leads didn't say no, but they didn't say yes either. They slipped between the cracks or faded into the background. Reach out to them. For example, you could have your sales team call them and politely ask if they still have a need for your product or service. After all, something prompted them to raise their hands in the first place.

7. **Joint venture:** What other products or services do your customers need? When you create a client, who else do you create a client for? Who creates clients for you? Strategically search for win-win ways to pool resources with high-integrity, trusted joint venture partners in complementary businesses.

8. **Buy or sell dead, stale, or sated leads:** Dead leads are those that ended in a clear no. Stale leads are those that petered out without a clear yes or no decision. Sated leads are those clients who have already bought everything you have to sell them and would be a strong lead for another business. Either buy these types of leads from your competitors or sell yours to your competitors or joint venture partners.

9. **Reciprocal lead exchange with your competitors:** Trade your dead, stale, or sated leads for a fair number of your competitor's. Provided you track your results, everyone wins. Catalog companies do this all the time. They pool their mailing lists through a third-party broker who allows companies that share 100,000 names to get 100,000 names in return. How could you apply this concept in your business?

10. **Unconsummated transactions:** An unconsummated transaction is any client order that got stalled or interrupted. For example, it could

be a "dropped cart" in your website or a phone call to your sales team that got interrupted. Examine your business. Where are most of your sales made (e.g., online through a website or in person via a field sales person)? What's the most common way your sales process gets interrupted? How can you measure how often this happens and how much it costs your business? Once you determine if the cost is great enough to warrant the energy, develop a system to save these sales and track its efficacy. For example, in the case of dropped carts, you could program your system to automatically log any dropped cart it can track. If the sale amount is less than $200, have your system send an automated email apologizing and offer that same item at a discount or add a bonus. If the sale amount is more than $200, have a live sales rep call the customer to *"personally investigate where our system failed you and do our best to make it up to you."*

11. **Refer out:** What other types of products or services do your clients need that you don't provide? Where else could you refer them to purchase these products or services? Arrange a referral fee or a percentage of sale or, at the very least, a reciprocal referral program.

12. **Formal referral program:** Your best "salespeople" should be your customers and clients. How can you empower and incentivize them to send others to your company? Do you have a referral system in place that your sales team uses to proactively ask for referrals from your clients at least twice a year? The ideal time to ask for a referral is the moment after your client has told you how much they benefited from your product or service. You can improve your referral results by priming your client with a cue to know who you want them to refer to you.

For example, in Maui Mastermind we ask our clients, *"Who are three other business owners you know who are looking to take their business to the next level? These three business owners are probably tired of working for their businesses instead of having their businesses work for them and they would love to have a concrete road map and upgraded peer group to help them make their business more successful."**

---

*If you've gotten great value from this book or the Maui community and you know of business owners who fit that description, please share this book with them. Refer them to **www.MauiMastermind.com** to check out resources. Or, buy them a copy of this book and mastermind together as you all grow your businesses to Level Three!

Pillar 2: Operations

Your Operations Pillar is the part of your business that creates the products or delivers the services your business offers, fulfills promises made by Sales and Marketing, and performs the general and administrative back-end functions of your business.

No company will thrive without having a well-organized, strong Operations Pillar. Sure, you can generate sales, but unless you're able to fulfill on the promises you've made, your business won't last.

The Biggest Operational Challenge Level Two Business Owners Face

The most difficult operational challenge Level Two business owners face is their ability to intelligently work themselves out of the day-to-day operations of their business. Too many Level Two business owners struggle to leave this area alone. Instead, they micromanage it, making it dependent on their continued involvement.

To reach Level Three, you have to intelligently let go of this area of your business, replacing yourself with sound systems, business controls, and scalable solutions so your business can do an excellent job of keeping its promises to your customers and clients.

Building Your Master System

Of the many steps to effectively build your Operations Pillar, the first is to build a draft of your master system—your system of how you will store, organize, access, and update all your systems. We call this master system your UBS.

David's Story

Fifteen years ago when I was hard at work building my first successful business, my partner and I came up with the idea of creating a company that would be independent of both of us. Although I hadn't developed the language and finer distinctions of a Level Three business, in essence, that's what we were attempting to build.

We laid out our dream on an over-sized sheet of white poster paper (which I still have in my archive) calling it our "Business System."

(continued)

David's Story (continued)

When we abbreviated that two-word phrase, we ran into a little trouble so we quickly added the word "Ultimate." Now we had the acronym UBS.

Our UBS (Ultimate Business System) was the collection of processes, procedures, checklists, and other systems we spent the next five years refining. In fact, in our company, UBS became both a noun and a verb. We'd say things like, *"Great idea to lower costs, Paige. Can you please add that to the UBS so that other team members can use it?"* It was a verb when we used it to say things like, *"Beth, can you please UBS that process so we don't have the same problems next time?"*

UBSing became a discipline and obsession in our business, and it's one I strongly urge you to adopt for your company. It's a philosophy of capturing winning processes and best practices into repeatable, scalable systems. It's also a clear structure within which to organize and house your growing collection of business systems.

The 5 Steps to Create Your UBS

You won't be building your UBS all in one sitting. Remember, building systems is an iterative process done over time. It will probably take 30 days to create the first draft of your UBS. After that, expect to edit and improve it repeatedly. What matters is not that you get it perfect, but that you develop the discipline of building and using systems within your company.

Here are the five steps to creating your UBS (after which we go into each step in more detail):

1. Break down each of your company's five pillars into its functional responsibilities.

2. Organize these responsibilities into subcategories so you have a clear hierarchical structure to organize your company systems.

3. Brainstorm the systems you already have and those you'll ultimately need for a fully fleshed-out UBS.

4. Triage the list of systems you need so every 90 days you have a prioritized list of systems to build.

5. Choose the technology you want to store, update, and access your UBS.

1. Break down each of your company's five pillars into its functional responsibilities.
Every business can break each of its five pillars down into its constituent parts.

Example: Acme Consulting, Inc.—Operational components:

- Consultant scheduling (to get the right team members on the right jobs at the right times)
- Consultant services performed (the actual "work" of the business)
- Client support (answering questions, solving problems, and building relationships)
- Coordination with Sales/Marketing (to take handoffs from the sales people and later hand clients back so they can expand client relationships)
- Coordination with Finance (to bill and collect in an accurate, effective, and timely manner)
- Back-office administration (to keep the office open, the phones and T1s working, and the filing systems and document storage organized)
- Technology (to keep the company's servers running, the websites operating, and the computer systems and network humming)
- Etc.

What are the functional components of your Operations pillar? Do the same thing with the other four pillars of your business.

2. Organize these responsibilities into subcategories so you have a clear hierarchical structure to organize your company systems.
Imagine you're writing the "Table of Contents" for your UBS.* Look at the following sample table of contents for a hypothetical company's UBS.

---

*To download a FREE PDF worksheet template you can use to create your own UBS, simply go to **www.MauiMastermindBook.com**. See Appendix A for details.

Sample UBS Table of Contents

1.0 Sales and Marketing
    1.1 Lead Generation
        1.1.1 Online
        1.1.2 Joint Venture/Referral
        1.1.3 Etc.
    1.2 Sales Team
    1.3 Lead Conversion
    1.4 Sales Planning and Strategy
2.0 Operations
    2.1 General Admin
        2.1.1 Office
        2.1.2 Etc.
    2.2 Website
    2.3 Consulting Services
    2.4 Purchasing
3.0 Finance
    3.1 Accounting/Reporting
    3.2 A/R
    3.3 A/P
    3.4 Budgeting and Planning
    3.5 Financial Controls
    3.6 Cash Flow Management
4.0 Team
    4.1 Hiring and Orientation Processes
    4.2 Training, Review, and Retention
    4.3 Compliance
    4.4 Outsourcing
    4.5 Exit Processes
5.0 Leadership
    5.1 Strategic Planning
    5.2 Leadership Development/Continuity Planning
    5.3 Company Culture and Traditions
    5.4 Communication Companywide

3. Brainstorm the systems you already have and those you'll ultimately need for a fully fleshed-out UBS.
Your goal is to have a list of all the systems ultimately needed in your UBS to run your entire business. Don't worry about ever finishing this list; things will continually change in your business. Again, what matters most is that you draft out this step. If you have key team members, get their input about the systems needed for their respective areas. If creating this list seems overwhelming, don't let that stop you. Remember, in the next step, you'll prioritize your list of needed systems. That way, at any given time you'll have three top priorities to work on, never more.

4. Triage the list of systems you need so every 90 days you have a prioritized list of systems to build.
When building systems, the biggest danger is to think of the process as a checklist you go through only once, writing out procedures as you go; then when you reach the bottom of your list, you're done. It just doesn't work that way in the real world.

First, it's unlikely you'll have time to build your systems in one concerted effort like this. What's more, you'll probably make mistakes as you do it, so you'll need to revise and update your systems. Finally, your business is a moving target. Things change, systems become stale, outdated, and redundant. It's crucial to continually prune and edit old systems to bring them current. That's why we keep emphasizing systems *as a discipline* rather than a process you do one time.

With your list of systems in hand, you next need to prioritize items on that list so you invest your energy building the most important, highest impact systems *first*. The following questions will help you prioritize your UBS's table of contents to see which systems to build first. Be sure to repeat this process every 90 days, updating the systems you'd like to focus on for that quarter.

Prioritizing Questions
How does this system:
- add to our bottom line?
- save us time?
- lower our real costs?
- add value for our clients?

Which systems would help us:

- scale up fastest?
- grow our sales?
- increase our margins?

How much would it/does it cost us to not have this system in:

- time?
- money?
- lost business?

The lack of which system is:

- costing us the most money?
- causing the greatest waste in efforts?
- creating the most expensive mistakes with clients?

Which systems:

- are the easiest and fastest to create?
- could I get other people to create, such as team members, outside contractors, vendors?
- will give us the greatest return for the least amount of time and money?

Taking your answers to these questions into account, sort your business systems into the following:

A's: Only three allowed! These are the highest-value, highest-cost-not-to-have systems that you will build *first*.

B's: These are the next 5–10 systems that matter most—but only after the A's have been addressed.

C's: Someday systems—everything else. These have a place on the list, but until they become an A or a B, beware of investing time and money into building them.

> ### Secret Leverage Point to Getting to Level Three Faster
>
> Up to this point, it's as if you are doing all the work of creating your UBS. Here's the good news: *You don't have to do this all alone.* In fact, if your business already has a much better "process thinker" than you are, get this person to lead the project of creating your UBS. As for building your systems, the best leverage point is to enroll your team to build your business's systems with you. Your most important job is to cultivate the discipline of systems throughout your organization.
>
> What's the only thing even more valuable than having your systems in place? Actually having your team use your systems! And having the culture in which your systems get edited, pruned, updated, and expanded as often as needed.

5. Choose your technology to store, update, and access your UBS.
Every company needs to come up with its own way of storing its systems for its team to use.* Your UBS requires storage with the following four attributes:

- *Accessible:* It needs to be accessible—fast. Usually, this means it's accessible online, but it could be a paper-based system, too.

- *Searchable:* It needs to be easily searchable. People have to be able to quickly find what they want or they'll start to keep their own "cheat sheet" systems at their desks or on their computers. This would eventually mean your UBS won't house the best practices but be merely a procedural manual that no one uses.

- *Version Control:* It needs to be collaborative, which means all users need to be able to edit and improve the data. This requires having version control and also means being constantly pruned of outdated information and systems. Systems will change and grow, and if you

---

*Technology constantly changes. For a list of the most current technology solutions we know about that you can use for your UBS, including a simple, FREE web-based solution, go to **www.MauiMastermindBook.com**. See Appendix A for details.

leave the old one to live with the new, it will cloud the waters and make it harder for people to know quickly which systems to use and when. In many ways, the *eraser* is mightier than the *pen* for your UBS.

- *Security:* It needs to have secure features that allow you to protect your intellectual property both from outside parties and from internal misuse. Regard your UBS as one of your business's most valuable assets.

What matters most is that you map out the architecture of how your UBS will be organized. That way, no matter which software or hardware you use to store it, you'll have a good start on an organized, useful way to create, store, access, and refine all your business systems.

Pillar 3: Team

Your Team Pillar establishes how you hire, orient, train, assess, compensate, and if necessary, let go of your staff. It deals with your policies and procedures for team members and the legal requirements of working with employees.

To grow most businesses, you'll need talented team members to both spark and support that growth. Whether it's adding sales team members to increase sales or engineers to design products or accounting staff to keep track of the money, your company's greatest source of leverage is your company's ability to attract, hire, integrate, and empower talented, committed people to "play" on your team.

Too many businesses never tap into even a fraction of the true talents of their team members. What a catastrophic loss—one that their owners may never even understand. But not *your* business. Make sure you engage your team in helping build your systems and design scalable solutions.

Here are some of the key systems you'll need to build for your Team Pillar to function optimally:

- Hiring processes
- New team member orientation process
- Regular staff evaluation process
- Team training

- Compliance procedures for all applicable labor laws
- Troubleshooting and personality challenges
- Exit process both for friendly partings and expedited exits (e.g., firings)

Who should your first key hire be? Typically, for 40 to 45 percent of business owners, your first key hire will be someone to lead the operations area of your business—a practice manager, an operations manager, or a formal COO. For another 40 to 45 percent, your first key hire will be in sales and marketing. And for 10 to 20 percent, your first key hire will be in the finance area.

How do you know in which area to make your first key hire? Easy. Look at what you're best at and naturally drawn to, and then make your first key hire complementary to that. For example, if you're a sales/marketing leader, make your first key hire in operations, freeing up your time to focus on growing sales. If you're an operational, process-driven person, your first key hire will likely be someone in sales and marketing. And if your business has great complexity in the financial area—either because it's a capital-intensive business in which managing cash flow and financing are critical or because the cost structure for delivering your product or service requires accurate financials and budgets—then your first key hire might be in the finance area. Remember, to grow your company, you have to intelligently hand off parts of your business.

5 Action Steps to Successfully Make Your First Key Hire

1. **Determine exactly which roles your business needs, then write a clear description of:**
   - tasks the new hire will do.
   - qualities you're seeking in this person.
   - values that person must embrace.
   - personality and communication style needed to fill the role.
   - skills the new hire needs to have.
   - experience you're looking for.
   - 3 to 5 "must haves" for this hire (the key things that matter most about this position and the person you want to fill it; the rest are "nice" but not essential).

2. **Create and follow your recruiting game plan, which includes the following:**

   ■ Design a written "help wanted" ad for the position. If it's for an operational position, include clear and concrete details of exactly what you're seeking. If it's for a sales/marketing position, make sure your ad is short and concise. We suggest you have applicants respond by emailing a résumé, cover letter, and salary history. This allows you to quickly do a first-pass screen and save time.

   ■ Determine if you already have someone on your team who fits what you're looking for.

   ■ Spread the word among those in your extended network and share your "help wanted" ad with them.

   ■ List your ad online (e.g., Craig's List, Monster.com, local paper, trade journals, professional associations, etc.).

   ■ Create a list of companies in which you'd find your ideal candidate and call people you think might be a potential match. Ask if they know of anyone like themselves who might be interested in the job. (Many will have a good network and some may even be interested in the position themselves.) This simple yet powerful technique is used by many professional recruiters.

   ■ Use online social networks like LinkedIn.com to find potential candidates.

   ■ Consider hiring a recruiting company to help find the right person. (Although it's the most expensive option, it's often the least time intensive and most effective.)

3. **Review your candidate pool and do a three-step process to find the top three candidates for your final interview(s).**

   One: Quickly sort candidates via résumés, cover letters, and salary histories.

   Two: Phone screen the top 10 to 15 candidates.

   Three: Conduct an in-depth phone interview with the top five to seven candidates and select three to meet in person.

4. **Interview each of the three finalists.**

   You may decide to do more than one in-person interview. Take your time and get to know your top candidates before making your final choice. We strongly suggest you do this interview(s) with one or two other people participating. This allows you to observe more and worry less about questions to ask. Plan your questions in advance along with who will do the asking and roughly when. Use this list of questions as a skeleton for how the interview will go, leaving space for other lines of questions that come up during the interview. (Save your interview structure as a template to use for your hiring system!)

After each interview, debrief your interview team about the candidate. What were his or her strengths? Weaknesses? How did he or she rate on a scale of 1-10 on the three to five "must have" qualities or experience sets for the position? You'll find it gets hard to remember candidate one when you're talking with candidate three two days later, so take detailed notes.

5. **Hire your winning person.**

Once you've found your key team member, bring that person up to speed and transition him or her to take over that key area of your business. Stay focused on setting up your new team member to win. That means don't just dump all responsibilities and run, nor micromanage that person to death. Gracefully transition your new hire into the role so that after three months, he or she has taken on 80 percent of the responsibilities and by six months, 90 to 95 percent. Within 12 months, your new team member should "own" the role entirely.

6 Suggestions to Set Your New Hire Up to Win!

1. **Create a written transition plan** that includes communication styles, key benchmarks, major milestones, descriptions of successful outcomes, check-ins, etc.

2. **Walk the new team member through your business** as if he or she were a new customer, giving the person a sense of the products and services you offer. Provide introductions to a few of your clients. That will make the work ahead feel tangible and connected to the lives of your customers.

3. **Set aside time in the first 90 days to regularly be there** for training and answering questions. Personally introduce the new hire to your team members and explain who plays what roles inside your business. At a minimum, meet weekly for the first 90 days. Regard this relationship as an essential investment in your business.

4. **Make sure to systematize this orientation** so you capture all the knowledge you're sharing with this person. Do this in case you've made a poor choice; you want to get the benefit of all your work with the next person you hire. Make it part of this person's role to build these systems, especially if it's in operations.

5. **Check the person's progress monthly for the first 90 days**, then quarterly thereafter. Make sure you provide regular performance feedback, noting the things done well and suggesting improvements for the future.

6. **Examine how your new hire is working out at the 90-day mark** and use this evaluation as a chance to improve your hiring process. What questions did you wish you would have asked? What actions did you take that worked well? What would you change to make your hiring process even better next time?

3 Reasons to Hire Slowly

1. **Cash flow:** You need the cash flow to pay for key hires.

2. **Integration:** You have to give your business time to integrate key new hires before bringing on the next, and the next, and the next.

3. **Leverage:** You need time to learn how to work with and gradually leverage your key hires.

Rarely do business owners come to the plate with the talent of managing higher-level executives in their own companies. It takes effort and patience to cultivate this skill, so give yourself time to learn it well. Plus, while you're hiring these team members, you still have to operate your company, hence your free time is still limited.

Who You Need—A Level-by-Level View of Staffing Decisions

Level One	**You**
Early Stage Level Two	You + **admin assistants**
Middle Stage Level Two	You + admin assistants + **leveragers/doers**
Advanced Stage Level Two	You + assistants and leveragers + **leaders in 2–4 of the key pillars**
Level Three	You + complete team including **full leadership team**

So take it slow. We suggest not bringing on more than one high-level key hire every six months. This will give you and your business the time you need to integrate your new hire into the fabric of your business.

Pillar 4: Finance

The Finance Pillar of your business encompasses all the essential functions of collecting, tracking, distributing, and reporting the flow of money in and out of your business. It includes your billing procedures, collection practices, and accounts payable processes. It also includes all financial reporting from balance sheets to profit and loss statements to statements of cash flow. All of these help your management team make better business decisions.

At Level One and Early Stage Level Two, chances are you have few financial systems in place. *This is normal for a small business scrambling to survive.* At the very least, we suggest outsourcing your bookkeeping to a part-time service so your financial transactions are accurately entered into an accounting software program such as Quickbooks®. It's okay at this stage in your business to live with messiness; your main focus must be on establishing sales and developing your core operational processes. Just make sure this doesn't become habitual.

Entering Middle Stage Level Two requires putting your financial house in order. Whether you outsource your accounting to a part-time controller or have someone on staff full time, it's essential that you enlist help to organize the financial area and begin establishing intelligent financial controls that your business will need as it grows.

At Advanced Stage Level Two, you'll most likely have a full-time controller overseeing the Finance Pillar of your business. As you enter Level Three, you'll probably have a full-blown CFO (Chief Financial Officer) working for your business, not just a controller. What's the difference? A controller is expert in following the financial systems you have in place; a CFO is expert in helping you build them. A controller can help you make sure you have accurate reporting and can maintain your existing financial infrastructure; a CFO can help you with higher order financial thinking, such as running proforma analyses and managing your credit lines. A controller can help you execute plans in the here and now; a CFO will help you plan for the future. And as your business grows, you'll need the high-order expertise of a competent CFO.

Here is a simple chart that lays out *when* the average business will need *which* Finance Pillar team member based on its sales volume.

When You Need Which Financial Team Members

Gross Sales	Your Business's Need
$0–100,000	"Small time" part-time bookkeeper
$100,001–500,000	Expert bookkeeper (full or part-time)
500,001–2 million	Controller (could be outsourced)
$2 million-5 million	Full-time controller + part-time CFO (could be outsourced)
$5 million+	Full-time CFO with small staff

15 Cash Management Secrets to Guard Your Business's Cash Flow

Because cash flow is the lifeblood of your business, you must manage it wisely. Here are 15 cash management tips to help you protect your business's cash flow.*

1. **Beware of increases to your fixed expenses.** They are hard to cut if the business needs to. Wherever possible, build flexibility into your fixed-cost structure.

2. **Watch your business sales cycles.** Make sure you're not building up assets, inventory, or staffing at a time when business is about to slow down.

3. **Growth almost always sucks up cash.** The faster your growth, the greater your need for sources of capital to fund that growth.

4. **Cultivate fiscal discipline as a core company value.** Remember, symbolic choices you make or allow as the business owner will find their way into the culture of your company.

5. **Consolidate your purchases and negotiate better pricing.** This is especially important for companies that have gone through a recent burst of growth. Too often, they pay prices based on purchase volumes they far exceed. Also, regularly go back to your established vendors and analyze their pricing. Are you still getting a great value?

---

*To learn more about how to manage your cash flow and increase your profit margins, we strongly recommend you join us for the Business Owner Success Conference. You'll learn concrete strategies to lower your expenses, increase your revenue, and protect your cash flow. For details, go to **www.MauiMastermindBook.com**.

6. **Get competitive bids from vendors.** Even if you plan on staying with your current vendor, the fact that *they* know you're getting outside bids will keep their pencils sharp and help ensure you get better pricing.

7. **Train your staff to ask for and get discounts.** A short training course teaching your team members how to get discounts—plus consistently recognizing people who do this for you—pays off handsomely in increased cash flow. This one idea alone could reduce your expenses by 5 to 10 percent!

8. **Build healthy relationships with your vendors and, if needed, work out win-win ways they can help you get through a cash flow crunch.** They can be excellent champions to have on your side.

9. **Consider *not* prepaying too many expenses unless you're given a business reason to do so** (e.g., a meaningful discount). Sometimes, it's better to pay a little more monthly to guard your cash flow rather than pay for an expense in full up front.

10. **Having a cash cushion at the right time can let you seize a market opportunity or ride out a market lull.** Always work to maintain a cash cushion (some form of liquidity) you can tap into when needed.

11. **Lines of credit are great sources of liquidity to finance operations, but they can be fickle.** If your business relies heavily on short-term credit to finance operations, deepen your banking relationships by consistently and accurately communicating with your bankers. Bankers hate surprises more than anything. Also, plan your contingencies in case your credit line gets reduced or, worst, closed.

12. **When needed, cut fast and cut hard.** Don't stretch out cuts that are necessary; take your lumps and get on with your business.

13. **Don't confuse profits for cash!** Profits are an accounting term and accounting can be a deceptive science. For example, inventory costs you cash, but the cash you spend doesn't show up as an expense until that inventory is sold or written off, which could radically distort your true cash position. Many other accounting fine points can cause similar distortions. Remember, you cannot fund payroll or pay bills with profits, only cash.

14. **The faster you get paid from your customers, the easier it will be to manage your cash flow.** Most businesses carelessly get into

cash crunches because they let their receivables slip longer and longer before being paid. Do whatever you reasonably can do to bring in payments quickly.

15. **Pay attention!** As simple as it seems, just getting and paying close attention to your A/R reporting on a weekly basis helps your business collect thousands of dollars more on the money owed. The result? It increases your cash flow and improves the effective operating margins for your business.

Creating Systems to Collect More Accounts Receivable—FASTER!

Obviously, the ideal system is collecting full payment before you fulfill your product or service. But this isn't always an option for many companies that typically bill for work done or products delivered after the fact.

The reason most businesses fail is because they don't have enough cash to keep going. That makes sense when you consider how a typical product-based business works. The business pays to manufacture or purchase their products and then inventories them until customers purchase them. Buying that inventory ties up the business's cash and increases its risk (e.g., damaged inventory, obsolescence when upgraded, etc). And when they *do* ask for payment, most business owners never create a clear, measurable collections system that can be improved over time.

It's our belief that most business owners are simply uncomfortable or even afraid to look clearly at this part of their business. They bury their heads in the sand and passively wait to get paid. Many are even afraid of upsetting clients by asking for payment. They don't want to deal with it so they push it off onto their bookkeeper or another poorly equipped member of their team who has no training and no system to follow.

Case Study: Bill

One of our consulting clients, Bill, owns a service business in Colorado. When we began working with him on his Finance Pillar, it became clear he was losing tens of thousands of dollars each quarter simply because he didn't have a reliable process of invoicing his clients. When we discovered all the past work he *hadn't even billed his clients for*, Bill said, "Well, it's too late to send out invoices now because I'd upset them."

This is a common fear. We explained to Bill that not only would sending invoices with a letter and a phone call immediately after generate $30,000 to $40,000 in cash, but by *not* getting paid, he was increasing his odds of losing these clients. When people owe you money over a long time, they tend to disappear. When you respectfully and professionally ask for and collect payment from them, they tend to stay with you.

David's Story

When I'm working with a new consulting client who is struggling financially, one of the first places I examine is their A/R and their collections practices. Having done this for so long, usually I can help a business owner get a 5 to 15 percent boost in *collected* gross income within 90 days.

Think about this for a moment. If your business operates at a 33 percent profit margin, then that 5 to 15 percent increase in gross income actually translates into a 15 to 45 percent increase in net profit! That's the power of your Finance Pillar and why you *must* pay attention to it.

8 Tips to Lower Your Outstanding Receivables

1. **Consider the timing of your billing and collect up front.** If you can get paid before you fulfill your product or service, you can eliminate a whole lot of hassle and additional cost chasing down payments later.

Case Study: Dawn

One of our clients, Dawn, owned a consulting business. In the past, she typically got paid at the end of her consulting assignments. We coached her to ask for payment up front (or at least a partial payment up front with additional payments based on milestones met over the course of the project versus the end of the project). While this didn't work with all of her existing clients, a new client cut her a check for $225,000 for a project to be completed over the subsequent 12 months! You never know until you ask, so ask!

2. **Don't wait to bill.** If you can't bill before you fulfill, at the very least, give your customers a bill at the time the services are rendered

and ask for payment right then. Remember, the longer you wait to bill, not only the longer it is before you get paid but the more likely you'll encounter collection problems.

3. **Get your clients to prepay an entire year by providing an enticing incentive to do so.** Doing this helps your cash flow plus eliminates the need for the entire accounts receivable collection process. Incentives might include a special add-on bonus or a discount.

4. **If your business model must have accounts receivable, front load the collection process.** Send statements immediately and start your follow-up procedures right away, not after 60 to 90 days have passed. Put in that energy up front when your odds of collection are highest.

5. **When you ask for money, make it easy for your clients to pay you.** For example, include a self-addressed envelope. Make sure the invoice clearly says who to make the check out to, for how much, and where to send it. Accept credit cards. Set up autobilling.

6. **Build into your standard contracts a "carrying cost" for your clients who pay slowly.** If you end up financing your customers' purchases, then get paid for your trouble. Make sure your contract includes a monthly financing charge for all accruing bills. Ensure that it also states they're responsible for all reasonable costs of collection. Finally, where possible, get a personal guarantee from your customers rather than allowing the money they owe you to only be owed in the name of their entity.

7. **Be smart about the people you task with asking for payment.** By default, most companies assign their bookkeepers or controllers to ask for payment. But these people tend to have weak interpersonal skills. Instead, consider involving a mix of people in your business to collect what's owed. For example, when the receivable is fresh, ask your sales team to make collection calls. Because many of them are compensated on a commission basis, they have a strong financial incentive to help. Later, if you need to escalate the collections efforts, consider involving your legal counsel in the process. (See Case Study: The Paul Principle on the opposite page.)

8. **If you have to escalate your collections efforts, compress the timeline.** Don't let slow-paying customers stretch out payment for another 60 to 90 days.

Case Study: The Paul Principle

Most people who owe money are paying *some* of their creditors; you just need to make sure that you're one of them. As Maui Advisor and attorney David Bolls says, "Make sure that anyone who owes you money sees you as Paul, as in 'rob Peter to pay Paul.' No matter what, you want to make sure that if they are paying *someone*—and they probably are—they're paying *you*."

David works as the chief legal counsel for a large media company where he created a collection system for times when payment requests need to be escalated. He notes that most businesses that owe money try to stretch out the time before they either pay or admit they can't pay, some as long as 120 to 180 days! When you contact them for payment, they'll ask for a copy of the original invoice. When you send it, they say it might be incorrect and ask for a more detailed invoice breaking down the charges. Then they say they didn't receive that and ask you to send it again. On and on the delaying tactics go.

In David's company, when a client hasn't paid, here's what happens. First, the sales team is brought in to "sell" the client on paying. If that doesn't get results, a complete "collections package" is prepared and sent to the client by certified mail. It includes a cover letter from legal counsel along with a detailed accounting for all charges, a clear invoice to be paid, and a copy of the completed court paperwork set up to file suit for nonpayment (unfiled at this point). Interestingly, David finds that when his company's clients receive this package, they realize nonpayment is *not* an acceptable option. Somehow they manage to pay.

In the event that clients ask to arrange a payment plan, David has them sign a clear, legal document (which is part of his company's collection system) that spells out their agreement and states that this is a valid debt. It also contains a provision that, in the event of default on the payment plan, this agreement is a "confession of judgment," thus saving time in the legal process of collections actions.

Other provisions in David's standardized "payment plan" agreement state that, upon default, all unpaid sums will have a high interest rate and that all reasonable costs for collection will be borne by the nonpaying party. Not surprisingly, this system has helped David's company collect tens of millions of dollars that might otherwise never have been paid.

Pillar 5: Executive Leadership

The final pillar of your business is Executive Leadership—the area that leads your leaders and sets the big-picture direction for your company. It's also likely the final area for you to personally let go of. Remember, many Level Three business owners choose to stay in their businesses as CEOs and continue working. The key distinction is that this is a choice; it's not a requirement for their companies' survival. Successful business owners groom their successors and ready their organizations to successfully transition leadership when they feel the time is right.   ·

As the leader of your business, you have these four main responsibilities:

1. Setting the big-picture vision for the business. This means clarifying your Vision, Mission, and Values so they become tangible and meaningful in the lives of your stakeholders. It also means establishing the direction and long-term objectives of your organization.

2. Defining the big-picture strategy to reach your business goals.

3. Growing, grooming, and integrating your leadership team.

4. Dreaming up what comes next. As the leader, you must keep looking toward tomorrow to make sure your business stays vibrant and relevant as the world—and your clients' needs—change. Complacency in a changing world is fatal.

On a macro level, your job as leader is establishing what your business stands for and how it "sees" itself—that is, where it's focused and toward what end it's moving.

Leaders create the narrative through which all stakeholders interpret the business and their relationship to it. *Meaning drives emotion; emotion drives behavior.* As you grow your business, it becomes increasingly more important that you shape the stories and traditions that will become part of your company's heritage. These hold your business on course even when you're no longer present each day to drive it.

On a micro level, you want to create a business in which all team members understand their roles, know what they're responsible for, how success in their role will be measured, and how leaders and team members will provide feedback as they go.

What Business Do You Want to Build?

Too many business owners get so caught up in the day-to-day running of their companies that they never step back and think through—on paper—

precisely what kind of business they want. One of your key responsibilities as the leader of your business is to create a clear, concrete, and inspirational picture of the business you and your team are working to build.

What business do you want to build over the next three to five years? What does it look like? What's your gross revenue? Net profit? Key margins? How many customers do you serve? What are the trends in these areas?

What about the qualitative picture of your business? Who are your team members and what are their qualities and roles? How do you measure the success of your business in the lives of your clients?

What do you anticipate your eventual exit strategy will be? What elements will you need to have in place to execute that exit strategy to greatest effect?

Taking time to clarify and describe the business you're working to build *up front* will save you mountains of time, energy, and frustration.

The Level Three Business Audit™

To get where you want to go, you first have to know your starting point. We've developed a proprietary assessment tool to help you determine your business's exact starting point. It's called the *Level Three Business Audit.*

This 128-question tool not only helps you strategically dissect your business and identify its strengths, weaknesses, and key leverage points, but it also places it in its exact location on the Level Three Road Map. We use it as the first step we take with any consulting client we accept into our program.

Let's go through an *abridged* version of this assessment so you can clearly see where your business currently stands. As you rate your business on these 30 areas (six for each pillar of your business), notice what your answers reveal about its position on the Level Three Road Map.

Score Your Business Pillars

Rate your business pillars in each of the six areas listed on a scale from 1 to 10 (with 1 being lowest and 10 being highest). For example, under "lead generation," if you think your business does a fantastic job at consistently generating new leads, give yourself a 9 or 10. If your business struggles to find new leads, barely generating enough to keep it afloat, give yourself a 2 or 3. Total your score for each pillar (possible high score of 60 for each pillar) and then total your score for the entire

(continued)

audit. When you're done with this mini audit, we'll explain how to use the results.

Sales and Marketing Pillar:

Lead generation _____

Lead conversion _____

Client repeat business _____

Client "upgrade" business _____

Revenue growth (current) _____

Future prospects for revenue growth _____

Total ═════

Operations Pillar:

General administrative function _____

Performance of client work or fulfillment of client orders _____

Client's rating of your company's performance _____

Cost controls for operation of your business _____

Business infrastructure (website, physical location, equipment, etc.) _____

Scalability of your core product or service _____

Total ═════

Team Pillar:

Communication systems for team to work together _____

Having the right team in the right positions _____

Systems for bringing on new team members _____

Systems for training and reviewing team members _____

All team members have a clear understanding of: _____

- What their jobs are.
- How they are expected to perform them.
- How their work will be measured.

(continued)

- How their work contributes to the bigger picture of the company's mission.
- How their work adds value to the lives of your clients.

Strategy and use of outsourced solutions   _____

Total   ══════

Finance Pillar:

Accurate and timely financial reporting   _____

Budgeting   _____

Financial controls   _____

Collection systems for accounts receivables   _____

Effective management and use of financing   _____

Cash flow management in general   _____

Total   ══════

Executive Leadership Pillar:

Each team member has a clear understanding of: _____

- The Vision, Mission, and Values of the company.
- The company's big picture goals, strategy, and priorities.

Current business strategy   _____

Review process for company performance,
direction, strategy, and development   _____

Troubleshooting major challenges when they come up   _____

Leadership training   _____

Company culture and tradition   _____

Total   ══════

Complete score for your business (scale of 30–300):   _____

Total your scores for each pillar and for your business as a whole. Don't worry; it isn't important that you score high now because what matters is not *where you start* but *where you end up*. And to end up where you want to be, it's critical to have a reliable way of evaluating current positions along the way. This abridged Level Three Audit is a simple tool to help you do just that.

If you have an **Early or Middle Stage Level Two** business, chances are your scores are currently quite low in three or more pillars. This is normal. You'll improve them rapidly when you follow the Level Three Road Map and mature your business. The two most important pillars at these stages are your Sales/Marketing Pillar and your Operations Pillar. If either scored below a 20 (out of a possible 60 for the area), then you have concentrated work ahead to improve these two critical pillars. At this time in your business, if you score low in reliably generating leads, closing on sales, and fulfilling on your promises, you need to immediately ·remedy that situation. *These functions are the minimum requirements to have a sustainable business.* Remember, basic survival is the first hurdle to get to Level Three.

If you own an **Advanced Stage Level Two or Level Three** business, chances are your scores in most pillars are high (above 40 for each pillar). Look for any specific pillar in which your score was below 20. It needs immediate attention.

You're encouraged to repeat this assessment twice a year. Make sure to date and save your scores so you can note your progress over time. It will give you a simple, structured way to score your business, know where it's progressing, and determine where it needs more of your attention.*

---

*To download a FREE PDF version of this assessment tool, along with a video training giving you more specific strategies to use it to accelerate your journey to Level Three, simply go to **www.MauiMastermindBook.com**. See Appendix A for details.

CHAPTER 5

6 Time Mastery Strategies to Free Up a Full Day Each Week to Build Your Business

Congratulations on making it this far in the book. By now, you have a real sense for the road map you'll follow when building a Level Three business and why, if you don't, you'll get caught in the Self-Employment Trap.

We just want to pause for a moment and share with you the two biggest excuses we've heard business owners use to settle for a Level Two life. (Remember, in life you buy into either your excuses or your dreams, but you don't get both.)

Business Owner Excuse #1: "I don't know how." Millions of business owners worldwide stay stuck in Level Two businesses because they don't know *how* to build a better business. This is no longer a valid excuse for you. You've been introduced to the specific methodology to build a thriving Level Three business. Besides, ignorance is just an excuse, not a defense.

Business Owner Excuse #2: "I don't have enough time to do this." Too many business owners point to their overly full days and say, *"See, I'm so busy doing the job of my business that I don't have time to step back and build my business."* That makes about as much sense as running full speed on an exercise treadmill and thinking if you run faster, you'll make it off the treadmill. The solution isn't to work harder; it's to get off the treadmill by working *smarter*.

Let's get real here. There's no such thing as having more time. We all have all the time there is. While we can change where we *invest* our time, we can't make more of it. The most successful entrepreneurs have learned to invest their time for the best and highest return for their businesses.

In this chapter, we offer six powerful time mastery strategies to up-grade the time you previously spent doing low-value activities to build the business you really want.

You don't have to work nights and weekends to build your Level Three business. Working longer hours is never the answer. Making better choices with how you structure your use of time is the best way to gain more time—both to build your business and just for pleasure.

Pop Quiz: 10 Hours of Time Guaranteed!

Would you like to participate in a simple exercise to gain an extra 10 hours or more each week without any extra effort or strain? Then we invite you to play along and answer the following questions:

How many hours do you spend *per week* on average doing the following activities?

___ hours	Watching TV
___ hours	Randomly surfing the Internet
___ hours	Doing low-value emails
___ hours	Doing office work you could pay someone $20/hour or less to do (filing, faxing, copying, typing, shipping, cleaning, etc.)
___ hours	Doing personal activities you could pay someone $20/hour or less to do (laundry, cleaning, yard work, simple repair work, personal errands, etc.)
TOTAL:	___ hours per week

If you're like most who take this pop quiz, you've probably found well over 10 hours a week that you could redirect into building your business if you made different choices. But heck, that was too easy, so we'll use that as a warm-up to the subject of your personal use of time.

As a business owner, you know that time is one of the most powerful variables you control in the success equation.

Many years ago, famed college basketball coach John Wooden said, *"It's what you learn after you think you know it all that really matters."* You'll get the most out of these tips on time mastery if you keep Coach Wooden's timeless advice in mind and approach this section of the book fresh.

Let's start by clearly stating we understand that, like every other business owner we've ever coached, you probably don't feel you have the time to do what we suggest. In fact, when we're working with a new consulting client, for the first six months, one area we focus on is upgrading the business owner's *personal* use of time.

What we've found—and what you'll find when you apply these six simple time mastery strategies—is that you can create 8+ hours a week to reinvest in building your business. In fact, our consulting clients average a savings of *12 hours a week*, which they redirect into other better and higher uses inside their business. For example, Wayne, one of our consulting clients in Oregon, used these strategies to free up an average of *15 hours* a week. This allowed him to reinvest in building his business, which for him initially meant building better sales systems and later meant building out his management team.

We're not asking you to work longer hours or nights or weekends. Far from it. Instead, we're asking that you consciously take charge of *how* you use your time, and focus it on the best and highest return for your business.

Before we share these six strategies with you, imagine for a moment that they worked. Don't you *know* that you could grow your business by 25 to 50 percent or more if you could just create an extra 1 to 2 days each week to step back out of the job of your business to focus on taking those actions steps that would grow and expand your business? Of course you could. That's why these strategies and techniques will make such an immediate and dramatic difference in your business.

6 Time Mastery Strategies

Time Mastery Strategy 1: To upgrade your use of time, first identify what you do that truly creates value for your business.

Time Mastery Strategy 2: To "find" the time, focus first on your D Level activities.

Time Mastery Strategy 3: Structure your week to reinvest your "saved" D time in A and B activities.

Time Mastery Strategy 4: Work "above the line" and live by the Results Rule™.

Time Mastery Strategy 5: Every "Push Day," schedule in a 60–90 minute "Prime Time" block during which you'll work on A or B activities.

Time Mastery Strategy 6: Create a "Stop Doing" List and add to it weekly.

Time Mastery Strategy #1

To upgrade your use of time, first identify what you do that truly creates value for your business.

As a business owner, you don't get paid for time and effort; you get paid for creating value. So as you build your business, look for ways to create value independently of putting in your personal time. This essentially is what it means to build a business, not a job.

If you've read anything on time management, you've come across Pareto's Principle, inspired by the work of 19th century economist Vilfredo Pareto. Commonly called the 80-20 Rule, Pareto's Principle says that 20 percent of your actions generate 80 percent of your results (high value) and 80 percent of your actions generate the other 20 percent of your results (low value).

This useful distinction becomes the basis of a refined model for using your time to create massive value, independent of the hours you put in.

If you take the 20 percent of your actions that generate 80 percent of your results and apply the same distinction a second time, then 20 percent of that 20 percent produces 80 percent of 80 percent of your results. That means 4 percent of your effort (the 20 percent of 20 percent) generates 64 percent of your results.

And if you can bear with us for one more math moment, apply this distinction one final time.

This means that only 1 percent (20 percent of 20 percent of 20 percent) generates 50 percent of your results! That's right; only a fraction of your highest-leverage work produces *half* of all your results!

We used this idea to create something called the Time Value Matrix™ — an actual formula to quickly and accurately quantify the "per hour value" of four distinct types of time: A Time, B Time, C Time, and D Time.*

D time is the 80 percent of unleveraged, wasteful time that only produces 20 percent of your total return. We call this the "80 Percent Mass."

C time is the leveraged 20 percent that produces 80 percent of your results. We call this "Leveraged Time."

---

*How you use your time is so critical to your success as a business owner that we've recorded a one-hour online workshop on these time mastery strategies. To immediately access this FREE online workshop, go to **www.MauiMastermind Book.com**. See Appendix A for details.

B time is the highly focused 4 percent that generates 64 percent of your results. We call this time the "4 Percent Sweet Spot."

A time is the top of the pyramid—the "Magic 1 Percent." Fully 50 percent of your results come from these activities.

Did you know that most business owners have no clue which of their activities fall into these four categories? So how in the world can you create more A and B time if you don't know what activities constitute A and B time for you?

Before we share with you some examples of our A-B-C-D level activities, understand that one person's D activity may be another person's A or B level activity—it's all relative. The examples from our business lives are illustrations that are not to be taken as absolute benchmarks of value. For example, one of David's D level activities is dealing with billing disputes. However, people in his company have this activity as one of their C or B level activities. Your A-B-C-D level activities are only comparable to you, not to other people.

Take action and examine what creates the highest value for *your* business at this moment in time.

Action Time: Identify your A-B-C-D activities and learn what you do that truly creates value for your business.

D Time: The 80 percent mass of unleveraged, wasteful time that only produces 20 percent of your total return.

Examples of David's D activities:

- Sorting mail
- Paying for and disputing bills
- Low level email
- Scanning documents into his electronic filing system
- Setting up phone meetings

List five of your D activities.

1. _____

2. _____

3. _____

4. _____

5. _____

C Time: The leveraged 20 percent that produces 80 percent of your results.

Examples of David's C activities:

- Delegating to his assistant
- Dictating a letter
- Holding a group meeting versus talking with several people one at a time
- Updating his master to-do list
- Sending out an email update to his exec team

List five of your C activities.

1. _____

2. _____

3. _____

4. _____

5. _____

B Time: The highly focused 4 percent "sweet spot" that generates 64 percent of your results.

Examples of Stephanie's B activities:

- Meeting with key clients to solidify the relationship
- Coaching her management team to be better leaders
- Sharing company stories/successes/challenges in her biweekly letter that accompanies team member's pay checks
- Reviewing her company's quarterly progress
- Instituting a systemic solution to a recurring problem

List five of your B activities.

1. _____

2. _____

3. _____

4. _____

5. _____

A Time: The magic 1 percent that generates more than 50 percent of your total results.

Examples of David's A activities:

- Making executive level hiring decisions
- Decision meetings with key joint venture partners to secure high-value, win-win strategic partnerships
- Making strategic decisions that set the direction of the business
- Holding the executive team accountable to their deliverables

List five of your A activities.

1. _____

2. _____

3. _____

4. _____

5. _____

Now that you've identified your current A-B-C-D level activities, it's important to understand that what you currently list as an A or B level activity will change. For example, if meeting one on one with a prospective client is an A level activity for you, make sure that in 6 to 12 months, you've increased the value you create for your business so this activity is pushed down to a B or C level activity. Ideally, working with a joint venture partner who can generate dozens of leads for you every month will become an A level activity, or training your sales team to meet with prospective clients one-to-one, or creating a sales DVD that generates passive sales. By that point, meeting one-to-one with a prospective client is no longer important for you to do personally. This is good. This is growth. And it's why your business becomes increasingly more valuable over time.

When you really get this distinction and shift your focus from "putting in hours" to *upgrading* the type of work you do (more A and B time and less D time), you'll find the results to be amazing.

Case Study: Gurpreet

One of our long-term clients, Gurpreet Padda, is a surgeon in St. Louis. He's also a serial entrepreneur who's had more than a dozen Level Three businesses. As you can imagine, his time is highly precious. Listen to Gurpreet share in his own words the impact of applying these time mastery strategies:

"I'm a surgeon with a thriving pain management and anti-aging practice. I'm also a serial entrepreneur with a dozen other businesses from restaurants, to medical billing services, to commercial real estate projects. As you can imagine my time is my most precious resource. Without question Maui's time mastery workshop was an incredible value, so much so that I got the home study version and proceeded to drive my office staff crazy as I listened to it every day for a month. But the results speak for themselves—the program helped me to radically upgrade my use of time and make an additional $1 million of net income. I still use these same strategies and principles to this day and find them just as useful and profitable. I don't see how any serious business owner could miss the opportunity to work with the Maui team and learn these and their other Level Three strategies. I've made the time to be at six of their workshops over the past several years, and this year I'll be returning for my fourth Maui Mastermind Wealth Summit."

Remember, it's limited Level Two thinking to believe that the solution is to work harder and longer. Instead, it's imperative to upgrade your use of time. For example, if you were an attorney who charges $300 an hour, what would your D time activities be? Things like fixing a computer glitch, making copies, sorting mail, or little things you can't bill a client for! And what would your C time activities be? Any time that's billable, like working on a legal brief, reviewing a contract, or updating a client on legal considerations.

Understand this: C time can provide you with a great income, but you'll always have to work exceptionally hard to earn it. This is the trap that catches most high-income professionals. They seek to increase their earnings by cranking out more hours. MISTAKE! Working more hours will only take you so far; it's just not scalable past a certain point (not to mention that when you get there, you'll be exhausted from so much work and a stranger to your family, too!).

The answer lies in A and B time. For this attorney, B time might include building relationships with other professionals who can refer valuable business, or putting systems in place so staff can get better results without tapping too much into the attorney's time.

What would A time look like? This could be speaking at a large conference where this attorney is able to generate new client relationships worth hundreds of thousands of dollars in billable services. Or it might be creating an accounts receivable system that increases the collection on all the firm's billings by 10 percent.

See the difference? You want to get D level activities off your plate; C time is needed to do your work more effectively. A and B time, however, are when you step out of the "job" of the work and do something that improves your capacity to create results, or significantly push back your biggest limiting factor (e.g., generating new clients, improving a critical system, etc.).

In fact, by upgrading your use of time instead of increasing your hours worked, you can often create huge business breakthroughs while still working fewer hours. Trading time for dollars is a Level Two reaction. Upgrading your use of time to create more with less is the Level Three solution!

So here's the big question: *How can you have more A and B time?* You won't get it by "trying harder" or by sitting down and saying, *"Okay, let's have an A moment right now."* Sorry, it just doesn't work that way. That would be like a parent saying to a three year old, *"Let's have an hour of quality time right now, Junior."* How well do you think that would work?

To get more A and B time, you have to fundamentally alter the way you *structure* your day and your week, which is exactly what the next four time mastery strategies will help you do.

Time Mastery Strategy #2

To "find" the time, focus first on your D level activities.

This one may seem counterintuitive, but the best place to look *first* to upgrade your use of time isn't your A, B, or C level activities. It's looking at your D level activities. Not only by definition do you spend a lot more time at this level, but it's the easiest place to make changes because consequences of dropping them are small.

So list all the D level activities you do on a weekly basis. Even keep a time log for a week or two so you can spot the wasted time spent on low-value D activities. Once you've identified them, you can apply the following "four D's" to get them off your plate.

The Four D's

1. **Delete it.** Some D activities just plain shouldn't be done by anyone. Look at the action item and ask yourself what's the consequences if no one did it. If it's small, then consider just crossing it off of your list altogether.

2. **Delegate it.** Maybe it's a task that needs to get done, but not necessarily by *you*. Hand it off to your assistant, or a staff member, or a vendor. Anytime you can hand off a D level activity to someone, you free up both your time and your focus to do more valuable work for your business.

3. **Defer it.** Maybe this task needs to be done and done by you, but should it happen right now? Sometimes delaying the action is the smartest choice.

4. **Design it out.** If you find yourself handling a recurring D activity over and over, instead of doing it, improve the process or system to keep the task from coming up in the first place. For example, if you get the same seven customer questions repeatedly, post a FAQ page with the answers on your website. Or perhaps you can preempt questions by giving new clients a "quick start" booklet that proactively answers these seven questions. Or maybe create an instructional DVD that gives new clients your best presentation while answering these common questions. You get the idea. Designing out a recurring activity is the very essence of building a systems-reliant Level Three business. It simplifies processes and empowers your team to get consistently great results with less and less reliance on you, the business owner.

So after you've identified what you do that truly creates value (your A and B activities), look closely at your D activities as the place to mine the raw ore of more time. By applying the four D's of Deleting, Delegating, Deferring, and Designing Out, you'll free up 8+ hours each week to reinvest in A and B activities. When you upgrade your time, you'll increase your sales, improve your cash flow, and dramatically grow your business.

Time Mastery Strategy #3

Structure your week to reinvest your "saved" D time in A and B activities.

It's not enough to free up 8 to 10 hours each week by clearing the clutter of your D activities; you have to fill your freed-up time with A and B activities. Nature abhors a vacuum, and if you don't fundamentally change how you structure your week, you'll find yourself squandering the time you supposedly saved on more D level "junk."

David's Story

Let me share a powerful concept to get more A and B time and minimize the D time that gets in the way. I call this technique "Focus Days and Push Days."

Mondays, Wednesdays, and Fridays are my Push Days. These are the days that I *push* key projects forward step by step. That's when I'm accessible by phone and email, and I hold many of my phone meetings. It's when I get the "job" of my business done.

Then I set aside my Tuesdays and Thursdays for my Focus Days. That's when I turn off the phones and email for the majority of the day, and I focus on doing the highest-value activities I can for my businesses (my A and B level activities). For me that usually involves writing: writing new books, writing sales copy, or writing business plans for my teams to implement. It can also involve holding high-value meetings or being in the studio recording a new business owner home study course.

On my Focus Days, I often leave the office and work remotely. Sometimes I go to a café or library and work there. Getting out of my normal environment removes the temptation to do the C and D level work that lives in every corner of my office.

Here's the most amazing part. Three to four hours on my Focus Days can result in more value to my business than *an entire week* living in C or D level activities. Focus Days give you a way to create the space in which to get high-value work done. (In case you're wondering, I do check in for 30 to 45 minutes at the end of the day to answer important phone messages or emails.)

Perhaps you can't set aside two full days a week as Focus Days, but you *can* find one day or at least *half* a day every week and use it as your Focus Day.

Action Step: Set aside one Focus Day every week. On your Focus Day, get outside of your normal environment and work on the highest-leverage, highest-value, highest-return part of your business. Do the A and B level activities that add real value.

This could mean building out a baseline operational process to use with new clients. Or you could spend the day creating a hiring system to consistently supply you with quality team members for your sales team. Or you might call on your two most important prospective customers or joint venture partners to deepen the relationship or close the sale.

The key is to set aside a full day a week for this and make sure your team supports you in keeping this time clear so you can invest in these high-leverage activities.

Decision Time: What day will you make your Focus Day?

"My Focus Day will be _____."

Time Mastery Strategy #4

Work first "above the line" and live by the Results Rule™.

Most business owners start each day with high hopes. They take a moment to write down the list of tasks for that day—a list that often grows to 15 or 20 items. But then the day hits and they find themselves pulled off track to deal with customer challenges, operational fires, or sales emergencies.

Here is a different way to organize each day.

When you sit down in the morning (or the night before, if you prefer), choose three bottom lines for that day and write them at the top of your to-do list. Draw a line under them to visually mark them as different and special. Make two of them business related and one of them personal. Your bottom lines are the action steps you'll take that day that will create the most value for your business. Almost always these are A and B level activities. On the opposite page is an example of a time mastery to-do list.

Live by the Results Rule

By 10:30 A.M., you should have either completed each of your three bottom lines or have scheduled a definite appointment time to complete them. We call this the "Results Rule." This technique is powerful because it pushes you to do what matters most *first*.

Most business owners put off these bottom lines to deal with the urgent requests that come at them during the day. In doing so, they sacrifice far more than they'll ever know. And Mastery Strategy #4 only gets better when you combine it with Strategy #5.

Sample Time Mastery To-Do List

1. Draft the marketing calendar for Q1.
2. Call Tom Smith about expanding joint venture.
3. Write my wife a love letter.

Email Shirley.

Check on Collin's project status with Angela.

Review web PPC proposal.

Call Larry (webinar glitches).

Call Jenna (her event questions).

Etc.

Time Mastery Strategy #5

Every "Push Day," schedule "Prime Time" to work on A or B activities.

Everyone has a certain time in the day when they're at their best. A Prime Time block is a 60 to 90 minute appointment that you set for yourself for your peak effectiveness time. That's when you work only on your highest-value items (usually your "bottom lines" for the day). By blocking out this time as an actual appointment on your calendar, you guarantee yourself at least one hour each Push Day to have a focused block of time to create real value for your business.

David's Story

For me, I make my Prime Time in the morning from approximately 8:30 until 10 every Monday, Wednesday, and Friday, which are my Push Days. I accept no inbound phone calls or emails during my Prime Time unless I deem that email or phone call to be the highest use of my time.

Certainly I'm not perfect, and at times I struggle with this strategy, especially because of the urgency and seductiveness of email. But

(continued)

David's Story (continued)

when I stay on target (currently about 75 percent of the time), it makes a huge difference in the value I get from my day. You'll find that setting aside this regular appointment to do your highest value work allows you to create more value for your business.

Time Mastery Strategy #6

Create a "Stop Doing" List and add to it weekly.
Too many people live their lives based on a to-do list to which they keep adding more and more tasks. But they rarely make the hard choices of what to let go of, what to delay, what to delegate, what to delete altogether.

Look at your to-do lists from the past 60 days. Which activities can you add to your "stop doing" list and how much time will that save you? Each week, pick a few more activities you deliberately choose to add to your "stop doing" list. You'll find that the items you put on it tend to be tasks you find draining—maybe ones you put on your to-do list out of obligation or inertia. When you get rid of them, you'll enjoy a sense of elation and energy plus have a much higher performance level in your other time.

The Real Secret to Unshakable Time Discipline

Most people shudder when thinking about a need for greater discipline because they've always associated it with pain and effort. But this isn't accurate. Instead, we suggest that you link discipline to two very important concepts: Accountability and Environment.

Discipline Is One Part Accountability
What person do you turn to who will hold you accountable for your actions and decisions within your business? Who coaches you to help you develop as a business owner? Who helps keep you on track? If you want to build a Level Three business, it's vital to have an accountability structure.

Remember, on your own, you are vulnerable, but connected with a peer group and advisor team who can give you feedback and accountability, you are unstoppable.

Discipline Is One Part Environment

Discipline also results from working in a structured environment. By controlling your environment, you make healthy, profitable behaviors for your business much easier. Remember, will power can win a sprint, but rarely a marathon. To win the marathon of building a Level Three business, take control of your environment to ensure it supports your goals each day. This means eliminating distractions on your Focus Days and during your Prime Time.

David's Story

I happen to be a chocoholic. I love chocolate anything. If chocolate cake, ice cream, or cookies lurk anywhere in my house, I eat them up. So how have I learned to structure my environment to support my health goals? Simple. I don't bring chocolate into my home. I don't allow it. If it's not there to tempt me, then it's much easier for me to maintain my health goals. I rarely bring any food into my home that isn't healthy.

The same lesson of discipline applies to my business. As mentioned earlier, I use Tuesdays and Thursdays for my Focus Days. I've learned that if I stay in my office for my Focus Days, I'm tempted to do C and D activities. That's why I usually step into a conference room or head out to a café or library to work. Because I've controlled my environment to make distractions unlikely, it's almost impossible to get sidetracked by an interruption on my Focus Days.

In the next chapter we examine the three biggest obstacles to reaching Level Three—and how you can blow through them!

6

The 3 Biggest Obstacles
to Reaching Level Three

What do you think stops you from taking your business to the next level? Daily demands of one crisis after another? Lack of cash to grow your business? Tough economy?

Ask yourself this question: *What have been the real roadblocks keeping me from growing my business to Level Three?*

Over the past decade, we've helped more than 100,000 business owners make their businesses more successful. During this extended time, a distinct pattern has emerged about what it *really* takes to build a thriving business. Initially, the specific pattern that emerged surprised us.

Once upon a time, we thought business success was determined by things such as your level of education. But it's not. We know hundreds of business owners who barely made it out of high school yet still built hugely successful businesses. For example, Peter, a serial entrepreneur we once worked with, struggled academically all through high school and never went to college. Yet today he's in the top one percent of all successful business owners in the *world*. Not bad for a guy without a college education! Remember this: at the upper end of success, formal education in no way predicts business success.

Also once upon a time, we thought business success depended on choosing the right industry to go into. But it doesn't. Thousands of people made their fortunes in mundane, ordinary, and even looked-down-upon businesses. For example, our client, Tom, made a *fortune* selling scrapped computer parts! And another client, Kathleen, made her fortune selling all-natural health care juices. Neither of these could be called "glamour" industries.

You see, these factors aren't at the root of why some people build successful Level Three businesses and other people stay stuck at Level Two despite all their hard work.

After diving deeper into the analysis of our clients' results over the past decade, we've uncovered three major obstacles that you must overcome to take your business to Level Three. If you don't successfully deal with these three obstacles, you'll be forever locked into settling—settling for less than you can earn, settling for less than you deserve, and settling for less than you were meant to have.

This chapter explains these three business obstacles and how to blow through them to reach Level Three. Business owners who've gone on to enjoy the wealthiest lives (financially and otherwise) have *all* found ways to overcome these three obstacles. Your failure to effectively deal with even one of them relegates you to a Level Two life.

Obstacle #1: Isolation

Without question, one of the common frustrations we hear from our most successful clients is that before they built up their peer group of like-minded business owners, they felt isolated in their business lives. Sure, they might have had people working for them, but they didn't have ready access to a peer group of other business owners with whom they could talk openly. This caused them to struggle, doing too much on their own. Only after they connected with peers and advisors who understood what they were trying to build could they get the perspective, support, and accountability they needed. That's when they finally made their biggest business breakthroughs.

Case Study: Stephen

Listen to how Stephen, a long-term client, described how he's been able to overcome the road block of isolation:

"Before I got involved with the Maui community of business owners, I had really isolated myself. I felt uncomfortable sharing my successes with my family and friends because too often that led to envy and jealousy on their part. It was just easier to keep that part of my life to myself.

"I also felt reluctant to share my failures with them because it never seemed to get me actionable and useful ideas to solve these

challenges. I wasn't looking for sympathy or a pity party. Rather, I desperately wanted a group with whom I could openly share my challenges, brainstorm ideas to solve them, be held accountable, and celebrate my successes. By reaching out and connecting with an upgraded peer group of other business owners and advisors within the Maui community, I've been able to bridge this gap and access great resources to help me succeed. Doing things on your own isn't only the hardest path to take, it tends to be the slowest, most expensive, and most painful route of all. Alone you are vulnerable, but connected with the right peer group and advisor team, you can enjoy the level of success you've always wanted."

Doing things on your own isn't only the hardest path to take, it tends to be the slowest, most expensive, and most painful route of all. Alone you are vulnerable, but connected with the right peer group and advisor team, you can enjoy the level of success you've always wanted.

Case Study: Blake

Blake was the typical Middle Stage Level Two business owner—isolated and building his business in his own little world. This former Army major had built a successful IT business in Colorado, but was stuck in the Self-Employment Trap. He desperately needed fresh insights and outside perspective and structure to help him take his business to the next level. Here's how he describes his business's transformation once he became involved with the Maui community of business owners:

"I've been working with you and the Maui team as part of the consulting program now for just over six months. During that time, I've completely upgraded the road map I'm using to build my company. Before we started working together, I was the typical Middle Stage Level Two business owner. I was making a really good income, but I also knew that if I ever stopped working, the money would stop because even though I had a few staff members, all the real work of the business ended up coming back through me.

"No more! I finally have a clear, concrete road map to build the business I really want to build. Not only do I have a plan and

a path to follow, I finally know that I can reach the point where the business's success will not depend on me day to day, if at all.

"Our sales are up, our collections have increased, and we're making more money than ever. My clients are happier and more satisfied with our service My company is barely recognizable compared to one year ago. Best of all, I finally see a clear map to scale my business."

The very real edge is having the right support structure in place. Can you imagine how much faster you'd reach your goals if you were a part of an elite community of business owners who supported you every step of the way? Take an honest look at your immediate peer group. Can you turn to these people to get the feedback and ideas you need to take your business to the next level? If not, how will you grow your network and upgrade your peer group?

5 Ways to Upgrade Your Peer Group

1. **Get involved with a local trade association, business owner group, or networking group.** This could be your local Chamber of Commerce, a local networking group, or the local chapter of a national trade association. The key is to become involved networking with other business owners who want to learn, grow, and expand their business visions.

2. **Attend one of our three-day *Business Owner Success Conferences* or other business owner events.** Not only will you get to network with an upgraded peer group of successful entrepreneurs, but we'll put you into a mastermind group and give you a clear template to develop and mature your mastermind group. (Go to **www.MauiMastermindBook.com** for a calendar of upcoming events you can attend.)

3. **Cultivate the mentors and advisor team to give you objective feedback.** This could be local business owners you informally cultivate to work with you, or it could be a structured program that you invest in and formally join.

4. **Get involved with a charity organization that both speaks to your heart and puts you next to other business owners.** This helps you build relationships and meet people who share your values of service and contribution.

5. **For the highest achievers out there, apply to join us in Maui for the annual Maui Mastermind Wealth Summit.*** You'll spend a full week in paradise with an elite group of business owners committed to playing the game of business and life at the highest level.

Obstacle #2: Fear

The second obstacle standing in your way of reaching Level Three is Fear. Fear can take on many forms: fear of failure, fear of success, fear of the unknown. . . .

Fear is normal and should be expected. Unfortunately, we've been trained that fear signals danger and you should either run away or fight. But fear is also a signal that you're stretching and growing. Anytime you do something beyond what you've done in the past, it's perfectly normal for you to feel anxious or afraid. One of the greatest business skills you can ever develop is learning to be comfortable with feeling *un*comfortable; learning to not be so afraid of feeling afraid. The key isn't to get rid of the fear, but rather to learn to take action in the presence of your fears.

Case Study: Kelly

Take the example of Kelly, a six-time Maui grad. When Kelly and her husband, Rob, first came to one of our events, they were police officers for the Los Angeles Police Department with $77,000 of credit card debt. Going to the event wasn't just a stretch for her; it was a gigantic leap of faith. At the event, she met other business owners who encouraged her to follow her dreams by starting her own business.

When her fellow officers learned she'd be leaving the force to start her own business, many of them said, *"You'll be back."* But when results showed up in that first year—so strongly that her husband also quit the force—her former co-workers said, *"You're just lucky."* Then after they saw her succeeding over time, something interesting happened. They changed their tune and began saying, *"We always knew you could do it, Kelly!"*

---

*To find out more about the *Maui Mastermind Wealth Summit* and apply to be invited to participate, simply go to **www.MauiMastermindBook.com** and click on the "Wealth Summit" link.

Of course, the reason she was able to succeed in those early years—besides tapping into an upgraded peer group—was because she faced her fears. She stepped up and followed input and coaching from the Maui Advisors. She also took massive action and consistently built relationships with her fellow Maui grads. The results speak for themselves. In the five years since first attending, Kelly has built a wildly successful health business and she completed several large commercial real estate deals including buying a 216-unit apartment complex and a second 156-unit building. Her businesses today generate 10 times more net profit than she used to earn working full time on the police force. Best of all, she and her husband have the freedom to spend time with their three toddlers.

How did Kelly go from $77,000 in debt to being a millionaire with several successful businesses generating huge cash flows? She did it by repeatedly getting herself to do the things that scared her. Can you imagine how frightening it must have been to leave the "security" of her job (if you can call being an LA police officer "secure") and start her first business? But she took action in the presence of her fears, and that changed her life forever.

How Is Fear Stealing Your Future?

Most people let their fears rob them of their futures. When they give in to them, they give up on their dreams. The saddest part is that fear doesn't only cost *them*; it also hurts the people they love most. It diminishes them as a role model for their children. It saps their family from so many opportunities.

So what's the biggest fear stopping *you*? Maybe you're like Thomas, a three-time Maui Mastermind Wealth Summit grad and consulting client. When he left his corporate job and launched his own business, he was terrified. He had to raise more than $400,000 of start-up capital (which he did) and move across the country to do it. But he kept focused on his dreams and took action despite his doubts. Now, the business he dreamed about is a reality.

Do you think Thomas could have even imagined he'd leave his corporate job and launch his own business *before* we first started working together? No way! But here's the key that has made all the difference for Kelly, Thomas, and every business owner in the Maui community: When you have a peer group of big thinkers and high achievers pushing and stretching you, anything—and we do mean anything—becomes possible.

David's Story

I've lived a lot of my life looking for ways to play it safe or not feel afraid. I've ended relationships because I was scared that other people would leave me. I've held myself back because I was scared of what it might mean about myself if I committed fully and failed. Over the past 10 years, I've taken a hard look at that part of me and made some major changes. One of the most important was the first of what's come to be known as my "Maui Commitments."

It was the second year we were hosting this annual business and wealth retreat, and I was having breakfast on a patio overlooking the Pacific Ocean in Maui. It was a glorious day and I was enjoying my morning feast, reading a local tourist magazine. One of the articles caught my attention. It talked about how you could scuba dive in the shark tank at the local aquarium.

A little background is in order here. I love to swim in the ocean, but ever since I saw the movie *Jaws* I've been terrified of sharks. I'd be out there swimming and I'd hear that "da dum . . . da dum . . ." in my head. I'd start to have a mild panic attack. Over the years, I'd learned to talk myself down from that, but it still was a huge fear for me. That morning, I decided I should do this shark dive and get over the fear. Notice the language there? "Should." Well, I conveniently let that idea slip from my head until the morning of the last day of the event. There I was, about to get up on stage and spend the morning teaching about how to make huge shifts in their businesses and personal lives when I knew I couldn't face them unless I walked my own talk. So that very morning, I made my first ever "Maui Commitment." I explained to them my fear of sharks and what it would mean to me if I could face it. I poured out my heart about how I was no longer willing to let fear rule me. I committed to them that by next year's Maui, I was going to swim with sharks. What a glorious moment it was, with people cheering and feeling inspired to make big commitments in their own lives.

But then I went home . . . and the thought of swimming in a tank full of sharks didn't seem so warm and fuzzy anymore. Besides, I didn't even know how to scuba dive! I bet you can understand what I did next. I procrastinated. I distracted myself. All the way up to six weeks before Maui rolled around again. I think part of me wanted to forget all about playing full out and just hide under the covers. Maybe I was hoping they would all forget. But I didn't forget. I knew it was important for me

(continued)

David's Story (continued)

to face my fear, to experience doing the thing I was terrified to do and survive that fear.

I made a call that day to make reservations for myself and a friend, Steve, a returning Maui graduate, to do the shark swim. In fact, I made the call from the parking lot of the community pool where I was about to undergo my second day of scuba training for certification!

The morning of the shark swim arrived and I was scared. Oh, I put on a brave face when I met Steve and his wife, Kim, that morning at the aquarium, but I was scared. I had just completed the final of my four "open water" dives needed for certification the day before. But I wasn't going to back out. Sometimes in life we need that accountability or a grand gesture that means nothing yet means everything. And so on that Friday morning, Steve and I slipped into that large tank filled with more than 25 sharks, including several hammerhead sharks and a 12-foot tiger shark. The first minute was all about remembering to breathe— deep breaths, one after the other. But a funny thing happened a few minutes into the dive. A switch flipped in my head from fear to fascination, from abject terror to amazement and wonder. These creatures were so beautiful and graceful. I left the tank that morning after 40 minutes of peaceful wonder. (And, yes, I had all my limbs intact!) I felt so empowered because I did the thing I feared most. Not only that, I found it was a tremendous joy.

As you progress in your business life and learn to play at bigger and bigger levels, you'll always find things to stretch and scare you. Embrace these opportunities and do the thing you think you can't. A whole new world awaits you each time you do.*

_____

*Would you like to see the exclusive video footage of David swimming in that tank full of sharks? Just go to **www.MauiMastermindBook.com**.

Obstacle #3: Hesitation

The final obstacle in your way to reaching Level Three is hesitation. You've gotten so much conflicting business advice over the years that you simply don't know which direction to move in. If you could only have a clear and straightforward plan to follow, you'd put in the time, talent, and creativity to build your business. It's just that you're afraid of putting in all the work and finding out later you followed the wrong plan.

But remember this—indecision kills! We know what happens to the deer that gets frozen on the highway staring into the headlights of an on-coming 18-wheeler! Standing still, stuck in the middle of the road, is the most dangerous place of all. Instead, you have to get moving. Wishing, waiting, and hoping will not get you to Level Three; only purposeful and directed action will.

Case Study: Kathleen

Kathleen, a four-time Maui grad, is one of nine children. Her mother had passed on to Kathleen and her siblings some of the limiting beliefs she'd picked up during the Great Depression. This "cautious" voice dragged on Kathleen, influencing her to make "safe" choices. But about four years ago, Kathleen stepped out in faith and launched a new business in the health field. She succeeded beyond her wildest expectations—and discovered that succeeding on a massive scale is also scary! But she held true to her vision of the business she wanted to build and the lives she wanted to touch, and she got herself to take the next step . . . and the next. . . . Today, Kathleen's health business has distributors around the country and nets her over $1 million a year in personal income. Remember, it's normal to feel afraid; it's a sign that you are stretching and growing!

Dealing with Your Blind Spots

All business owners have their own blind spots—those parts of their businesses or their behaviors or beliefs that dramatically limit their business's success.

David's Story

One of our clients, Dean, was a dentist with a thriving Middle Stage Level Two dental practice in Texas. But he'd had his practice 30 years and he wanted out. In fact, he was so fed up with the profession that he was literally ready to walk away from this

(continued)

David's Story (continued)

successful practice. As we worked with Dean, it became clear that he had to get out of the practice, but he'd never considered what he could do to sell the practice or structure it using the Level Three model. He was just too close to things to have the necessary perspective to see how, by following the road map over a short period of time, he could take his practice to Level Three. In the end it took him 12 months of hard work to do it, but he succeeded. Dean took a business he was about to walk away from and turned it into a six-figure stream of passive residual income.

We all have blind spots, and we all need outside advisors to help us see what they are.

Case Study: Dina

Many years before joining the Maui community, Dina had built a successful telecommunications company but had never heard of the Level Three concept and didn't how to build a Level Three business. When she wanted to get out of the business to start her family, she just let her successful business go. It wasn't marketable as a business because too much of the business couldn't operate without her to run it. This is how Dina stated that painful lesson:

"If I had gone to Maui Mastermind ten years ago, if I'd have known then what I've learned since from Maui about creating a Level Three business, I could have sold that business for millions."

Since then, Dina has learned exactly how to build a business that not only generates huge cash flow but is also saleable. Her blind spot 10 years ago cost her millions.

What are your "blind spots" costing you? And more important, *what are you going to do about them?*

In the final chapter, we'll walk you through specific action steps to turn the ideas in this book into tangible results for your business. Remember, to enjoy the rewards of Level Three requires the investment of Levels One and Two.

CHAPTER 7

Putting It All Into Action

Congratulations! You've made it to the final chapter—a real accomplishment. You've not only invested the time to read the rich array of business-building strategies and concepts, but more important, you've embraced the vision of building a Level Three business.

Now it's time for you to step up and apply what you've learned to take your business to the next level. In this final chapter, you'll find a three-layer action sequence specifically designed to help you accelerate your progress to Level Three.

Layer One: This book. In reading this book, you've gotten a clear picture of the Level Three Road Map, the best model to build a business not a job. You now have an excellent starting point for taking your business to Level Three. We'll give you several more concrete action steps to take in two more layers of the action plan.

Layer Two: The Business Owner Fast Track Program. We've spent thousands of dollars designing, testing, and refining this 30-day online business owner program. It will help you transform the ideas in this book into tangible results in your business as fast and as easily and enjoyably as possible. The program includes dozens of online training videos, downloadable PDF tools, and links to some of the best business owner resources on the Web. *And it's our free gift to you* because we believe you were born to make a difference, and reaching Level Three will give you more choices to have a deeper impact on the world.

Layer Three: Your real-world application of the strategies and concepts you've learned from us. Ultimately, it will be up to you to translate the ideas and road map we've shared into the Level Three business you dream of building.

Are you ready to take the final steps? We thought so! Let's do it together!

A 5-Step Action Plan to Apply What You've Learned

Step #1: Register for the Business Owner Fast Track Program.

Go to **www.MauiMastermindBook.com** or see Appendix A for details. We've arranged this *free* online program to help you take your business to the next level. Register immediately, then watch the orientation video. You'll get a quick overview on how to best use the program, so just follow the instructions. (Note: See Appendix A to get your *Access Code*.)

Step #2: Determine Your Business's Current Level and Stage.

Once you've registered for the Business Owner Fast Track Program, log onto the site and take the *Road Map Quiz*. This short, three-minute quiz will help you pinpoint your starting point. After you've taken that quiz, write your answer on the line below and date it. The date is important because it will become a treasured reminder of your journey's starting point as you follow the Level Three Road Map!

Business Name: _____

Current Level and Stage: _____ Date: _____

Step #3: Follow the Road Map for Your Level and Stage.

We've broken down each Level and Stage into its *three most important action steps*. Find your current Level and Stage and complete the given action steps.

Level One:

Focus: Creating your business plan and organizing yourself to launch.

Action Steps 1 and 2: *Clarify your business concept and conduct your market research.* Too many would-be entrepreneurs never come down from the dreamy clouds and actually come up with a concrete product or service to base their business around. Clarifying your business concept and researching the market turn your dream into a concrete target. (See pages 48–49.)

Action Step 3: *Write your business plan.* Remember you're writing only a *draft* of your business plan. It will always be a work in progress. The real value you'll receive from creating your business plan is sharpening your thinking and organizing your action steps. (See pages 49–52.)

Action Step 4: *Test market your product or service to see if it will sell!* Remember, ask for feedback from locals, not tourists! (See pages 52–53.)

Level Two Early Stage:

Focus: Securing your early clients/customers and becoming profitable.

Action Step 1: *Sell! Sell! Sell!* Execute your sales and marketing plan and win those early customers. You must secure these early sales to generate the cash flow you need to survive. (See pages 54–56.)

Action Step 2: *Begin creating simple sales and fulfillment systems to operate your business.* These can be sales and marketing tools such as brochures, scripted sales presentations, or a marketing calendar. Or they may be operational tools such as a staff scheduling worksheet, new client checklist, or store opening instruction sheet. Most important at this point is to start creating the rough systems that help you sell more and fulfill on the promises you've made to customers. You'll formalize and refine your systems as you mature your business. (See pages 56–58.)

Action Step 3: *As it makes financial sense, begin to build your team.* Remember the purpose of most early hires: to help you free up enough time to put your best efforts into growing sales and delivering on core customer promises. Each new hire should directly or indirectly help your company increase its revenues enough so this person provides a net gain to your company. (See pages 58–59.)

Level Two Middle Stage:

Focus: Building your business's core infrastructure.

Action Step 1: *Design and build your UBS—the master system of all your business systems.* (See pages 50 and 85–92.)

Action Step 2: *Build your most important core business systems and controls.* These include your baseline sales/marketing systems, your operational system to fulfill on your core product or service, and your key accounts receivable and cash management systems. (See pages 50–51 and 85–92.)

Action Step 3: *Refine your big-picture strategic plan.* Now that you've been operating the business successfully for a while, how do you plan to scale it? Download a PDF special report called *Crafting Your Business's Strategic Plan* by going to **www.MauiMastermindBook.com**. It will walk you through a simple process to create your company's strategic plan.

Level Two Advanced Stage:

Focus: Building your systems and cultivating your management team.

Action Step 1: *Refine your systems in your five pillars.* Each quarter, prioritize the systems your business needs and assign the creation of the top systems to your team. Remember to keep reinforcing the importance of systems thinking and use throughout your organization. Publically acknowledge team members you see doing a great job with your systems and quietly coach those team members who aren't. (See pages 85–92.)

Action Step 2: *Create a draft hiring plan for recruiting and cultivating your management team.* Your hiring plan will lay out which team members you'll need, when you'll need them, and how you'll go about finding them. At this point in your business, you'll need strong systems to hire, integrate, develop, and empower your management team. (See pages 92–97.)

Action Step 3: *Keep growing your sales.* As you build your business, maintain your focus on generating profitable business. Look for ways you can enhance your sales and marketing results by starving your poorest performing tactics and reinvesting the time and money in scaling your top producers. Also, make sure you choose scalable solutions when you update your strategy, and implement them in all five of your fundamental pillars. (See pages 78–84.)

Level Three:

Focus: Clarifying your exit strategy and executing on it.

Action Step 1: *Choose your desired exit strategy—sell, scale, or own passively.* (See pages 65–71.)

Action Step 2: *Create a written action plan to implement your desired exit strategy.* The most successful Level Three business owners give themselves a 12–36 month transition period to implement their exit strategy. This is why planning ahead for your eventual exit is so central to the Level Three Road Map. (See page 72.)

Action Step 3: *If you're planning to sell, insulate your business from your mental and emotional exit.* If your chosen exit strategy is to sell, it's critical that you keep a healthy share of your focus on running and growing the business. Too many business owners let their efforts to sell the business pull their attention away from their business, causing it to falter. If you plan on selling, we strongly recommend you watch the online workshop we've recorded for you called *How to Successfully Sell Your Company.* This 40-minute training is available for you at **www.MauiMastermindBook.com**. (See Appendix A for details.)

Step #4: Upgrade Your Peer Group.

Connect with the Maui community of business owners. Don't build your business in isolation. Reach out and connect with a peer group of ambitious, caring, high-integrity business owners who want to help you and receive your support and encouragement in return. Remember, alone you're vulnerable but connected we are strong.

Action Step 1: *Register for the Business Owners Fast Track Program at www.MauiMastermindBook.com.* This is your first step in connecting with the Maui community.

Action Step 2: *Join us at a live, three-day Business Owners Success Conference.* Not only will you learn how to grow your business but you'll be able to network with hundreds of other business owners equally committed to taking their businesses to the next level. Plus, we'll give you a concrete format for masterminding with other business owners. We'll even match you up with a mastermind team of five to six other business owners right there that weekend! (See **www.MauiMastermindBook.com** for details.)

Step #5: Remember Why You Want to Reach Level Three.

When you keep your burning "why" clear in your mind, the temporary challenges and bumps along the way don't feel so overwhelming. Go back to page 9 and review your top three reasons for building a Level Three business. Whose lives will you touch by holding true to your Level Three vision? Remember, your purpose needs to extend beyond just making money and feeling powerful. Your business must support your deeper values. How will owning a Level Three business impact your family? Your employees? Your community? How will it allow you to give more money and time to causes you feel deeply about? How will you be an inspiration to others? We grow wealthy by what we give. How will you share your good fortune on a bigger playing field? Remember, you can never really pay it back, but you can pay it forward.

A Recap of the 5 Most Important Points

We've covered a massive amount of information. Let's review the five key points we've presented for you to consider.

Point #1: Build a Business, Not a Job.

To enjoy the freedom and lifestyle you want, you must intelligently employ the four building blocks of all Level Three businesses: 1) systems, 2) team, 3) intelligent controls, and 4) scalable solutions. If you build for personal control, you're creating a trap for yourself. Instead, build your business so that one day it no longer needs your presence to operate successfully.

Point #2: Follow the Level Three Road Map.

You now understand the entire lifecycle of your business from launch to exit. Remember, at each Level and Stage you have distinct priorities and action steps to focus on. Follow the concrete road map we've laid out for you here. You don't have to reinvent the wheel!

Point #3: Build with a Level Three Mindset.

By holding a Level Three mindset as you journey through Levels One and Two, you'll reach your ultimate goal of a fully independent Level Three business much faster. Never again will you be satisfied with one-off measures; instead, you'll look for scalable, systems-driven solutions.

Point #4: Upgrade Your Personal Use of Time.

You *do* have the time to build a Level Three business. Use the six time mastery strategies you learned in Chapter 5. When you use the four "D's" to free up 5 to 10 hours a week of low-value D time, you'll be able to reinvest this time in your A and B level activities.

Point #5: You Can Do It, and the Rewards Are Worth the Effort!

Remember the story of Kelly who quit the Los Angeles police force to start her first business? Kelly went from $77,000 in credit card debt to an incredibly successful business in less than five years. If she can do it, so can you.

Or take Ryan, a client of ours for three years now. Ryan followed the Level Three Road Map but never made it to Level Three; instead, he sold his human resources company as an Advanced Stage Level Two business for $5 million! If you were to ask him if he ever thought he'd succeed the way he did, he'd be the first to tell you he struggled with the same doubts and fears you do.

Remember, feeling afraid is normal when you're stretching yourself and going after your dreams. It's a sign that you're growing.

If you ever doubt your capacity to stay the course and reach Level Three, then borrow *our* faith. We know you can do it. And you're not alone. Thousands of other business owners in the Maui community stand by your side. Together, we can support each other and accomplish our goals.

The world needs you to embrace your power and live your dreams. You'll never have the chance to relive this moment, so make it count. You are a gift in our lives, and we treasure you for it. Enjoy your journey to Level Three.

David and Stephanie

About the Authors

David Finkel. This ex-Olympic-level athlete turned business multimillionaire, is one of the nation's most respected business thinkers. A *Wall Street Journal* and *Business Week* best-selling author of over 45 business books and courses, including the wildly successful *The Maui Millionaires for Business*, his how-to business articles have appeared in over 6,500 periodicals across the United States. His weekly business owner eletter is read by approximately 110,000 business owners around the world. David is the founder of and CEO of Maui Mastermind®, one of the nation's leading business owner training and coaching companies. Collectively, David and the other Maui Advisors have personally started, scaled, and sold over $2 billion of businesses.

Stephanie Harkness is the cofounder and CEO of Pacific Plastics and Engineering. Over the past 30 years this serial entrepreneur has launched and sat on the boards of numerous start-ups, guiding them to successful exits. She is the former chairperson of the *National Association of Manufacturers*. The National Association of Women Business Owners awarded her the "National Woman Business Owner" prize, and Wells Fargo Bank awarded her its "Outstanding Entrepreneur" award. Stephanie has volunteered to be a Maui Advisor since 2007, paying it forward to other business owners and helping them make their businesses more successful.

The Business Owners Fast Track Program— Your FREE $2,275 Gift from the Authors

Attention Readers:

As our way of congratulating you for finishing this book, and to reward you for becoming part of the Maui community of business owners, we've created a unique online "fast track" program to help you immediately apply the ideas you've learned in this book.

We want to be clear here. We are giving you the tools and the road map to follow to take your business to Level Three, but you're the one who is going to have to do the work.

Are you serious in your desire to reach the next level? Are you willing to put the ideas and strategies you've learned in this book into action so you can enjoy the rewards of owning a Level Three business? Then we urge you to take the next step and claim your free $2,275 bonus right now.

To register, all you need to do is go online to **www.MauiMastermind Book.com** and use the access code:

Success101

When you register online you'll get immediate access to this comprehensive 30-day business owner fast track system. It's designed to help business owners like you master the ideas in this book, and to quickly and easily make your business more successful.

A Surprising Secret That Few Readers Know . . .

You may not know this, but the original draft of this book was over 90,000 words long! (That's 40 percent longer that our publisher wanted for the final version.) To be frank, it was heartbreaking to cut out so many business strategies and stories, but we had to do it anyway.

But since we aren't the type of people to let a small challenge like the space limitation in the book stop us from sharing all that we wanted, we decided to put all that extra content up on the web for you to get as a free bonus.

Actually, we didn't stop there. Rather than just give you the extra text, we took it to the next level and turned that extra content into a complete online fast track program that you get for free. Here are the details of what you'll get for a limited time as part of this special gift to readers like yourself:

What You Get as Part of This Valuable *Free* Bonus:

- **10 online business owner workshops** that will make building your business *easier* and *faster*!

- **Free download** of the business owner tools and worksheets from the book, including the business strategy template that we use with our consulting clients. Plus you'll be able to download several of our top business owner special reports!

- **Private access** to video footage from Maui and behind the scenes interviews with several of our top clients. Listen as they candidly share the things that helped them succeed, and learn how you can apply the same lessons in your business.

- **Comprehensive links** to the top tools, websites, books, workshops, and other resources for business owners like yourself.

- And much, much more!

You'll also Get *Instant* Access to 10 Free Online Business Owner Workshops:

Workshop One: How to Handle the Greatest Challenge Every Entrepreneur Faces!

Workshop Two: The 7 Sources to Secure Your Start-Up Capital! (And How to Pitch Your Deal so Investors Say "Yes!")

Workshop Three: Purpose, Passion, Position! (How to Make Your Business an Expression of Your Deeper Values)

Workshop Four: How to Create Your Business Plan!

Workshop Five: 12 Techniques to Leverage Your Mastermind Group!

Workshop Six: A Simple 5-Step Process to Make Great Hires!

Workshop Seven: Time Mastery Tactics for Busy Business Owners!

Workshop Eight: How to Reframe Fear and Use It to Grow Your Business

Workshop Nine: How to Pitch Your Deal So Investors Say, "Yes!"

Workshop Ten: How to Successfully Sell Your Company for Millions!

Best of all, you'll be able to attend all these workshops from the comfort and convenience of your own home! With a click of your mouse you can watch them on your schedule.

Here's How the Business Owner Fast Track Program Works!

Step 1: Go online to **www.MauiMastermindBook.com** to register using the access code:

> **Success101**

Step 2: Watch the introductory video training to see how to best use the program.

Step 3: Determine exactly where your business is on the Level Three Road Map™. There is a simple assessment tool on the website called the *Road Map Quiz* to help you pinpoint this quickly for your business.

Step 4: Follow the 30-day action plan that's laid out by Level and Stage for your business and take all of the FREE online business owner workshops. Also enjoy the other powerful business owner tools and resources that are available to you on this private website.

Step 5: Tap into the Maui community of business owners, both online and at our live Business Owner Success Conferences. Get involved networking and masterminding with other like-minded individuals so that together you can accomplish more than you dreamed possible. (Information on how is clearly laid out on the website.)

Register Within 30 Days and Get the Following Special Bonus!

When you register within the next 30 days of buying this book you'll get one more special bonus—a 60-minute video workshop with former Maui Advisor Jeff Hoffman as he shares with you a concrete system for reliably creating breakthrough ideas for your business. Jeff is an ultra successful serial entrepreneur who's built, bought, and sold billion-dollar companies. He was a founder and former CEO in the Priceline.com family of companies. This extra bonus is available for a limited time only.

Imagine watching Jeff as he shares his private formula for consistently keeping ahead of your competitors and scaling your business.
You'll learn:

- The 3 must have qualities of successful entrepreneurs!
- How to turn a one-time success into a repeatable process!
- The real reason to have a business plan (and why most business owners are missing out!)
- And much more!

How to Register for the Business Owner Fast Track Program—FREE!

Simply go online to **www.MauiMastermindBook.com** right now and complete the enrollment form. When prompted for access code simply enter:

> **Success101**

It's literally that easy!

Again, we thank you for reading this book. We wish you a lifetime of success and happiness. Enjoy your "graduation gift" of the Business Owner Fast Track Program!

Publisher's Note: This offer is for a very limited time only and we reserve the right to withdraw it at any time.

A Final Letter from David Finkel

What Would Happen to Your Business?

Dear Reader,

I have an extremely important question for you. One that—if you don't answer it adequately—could prove fatal to your business, ultimately destroying the financial lives of your employees and stripping away everything from you and your family that you worked so hard to build.

I don't want to be overly dramatic, but this is a very serious issue.

If you were hit by a bus tomorrow (or otherwise incapacitated), what would happen to your business?

For most business owners, the answer to this question is shocking. Studies show that if the average business owner was somehow incapacitated, their business would fold in less than 30 days! 30 DAYS!

Unfortunately, It Gets Worse . . .

Even if you're blessed with the health and good fortune never to be hurt or incapacitated, that doesn't mean you're home free.

The unfortunate reality is that most business owners are building a *job* for themselves, *not a business*.

The businesses they're building are dependent on them showing up to run them—day in, day out! They're what I call, "Owner-Reliant" businesses—with **long hours**, **no real freedom**, and **no defined exit strategy**.

And even "successful" businesses have to deal with this challenge.

In fact, because you're so busy doing the day-to-day *job* of your business, not only don't you have the time or energy left to grow and develop it as a business, **but you don't get to truly enjoy all the fruits of your labors!**

If you're not present each day your business suffers, in many cases grinding to a halt!

Are you really free if—even as the "business owner"—you don't control your time and what you do with it?

Isn't that the entire reason you became a business owner? To take back the control over your own schedule and enjoy the time freedom to do what you want, when you want?

How to Liberate Yourself from the Daily Grind of Your Business

If you find that you're stuck in your business there is a solution. At Maui, we call it the Level Three Road Map™.

It's the **step-by-step**, **concrete road map** we've developed over the past 20 years laying out the systems you need to develop, the team you need to hire, and the internal business controls you need to institute at each stage and level along the way to build a business, not a job.

If that sounds like a lot, well . . . it can be.

If you're looking for a magic bullet, the Level Three Road Map™ is not for you. It's for serious business owners who want to legitimately break through to the next level and build a business they can one day sell, scale, or even own passively.

Imagine tapping into this proven formula and system . . .

- No more guessing . . .

- No more struggling . . .

- No more doubting yourself or your decisions!

- Freeing yourself from your business so you can spend more time doing what you want to do (all the while your business hums along consistently generating value for the market and profits for you the owner—day-in and day-out).

- Actually feeling energized and having fun in your business again!

For years this is exactly what we've been doing—helping business owners just like you build a business, not a job.

And the most important thing of all is that we helped them do it by working *less*, and getting their *businesses* to produce more!

In fact, last year not only did **our average business coaching client grow by 36.42%,** but they also significantly reduced their business's reliance on them the owner.

We've included a brief overview of the Business Coaching Program, along with over a dozen reviews from actual clients sharing the impact the program had on their businesses. **If you're truly serious about reaching Level Three and want access to a structured, proven program to help you do it the fastest, easiest way possible,** I urge you to contact my office to learn how to get our help to take your business to the next level.

If your business qualifies, we'll schedule a **free 60–90 minute Strategic Business Coaching Session** with you and one of experienced coaches to look at your business, and exactly how you can grow it to the next level.

Sincerely,

David Finkel
CEO, Maui Mastermind®

P.S. Stop building your business in isolation and let our team mentor and coach you. Call 1-866-214-6619 right now!

P.P.S. If you prefer to apply online, just go to www.MauiMastermind.com/coach.

The Business Coaching Program

- A Concrete Road Map that Lays Out Exactly What to Focus On and When!
- One-to-One Coaching by Experienced Entrepreneurs Who've Done It!
- An Upgraded Business Owner Peer Group for Outside Perspective and Input!
- The Proven Support and Accountability Structure to Stay on Track and Scale Your Company!

How the Program Is Structured and Gets You Results

Layer One: The Strategic Layer—Planning, Prioritizing, and Sequencing!
Each quarter we'll work with you in a live, in-person Strategic Planning Workshop to make sure you have a clear, written 1-page plan of action to follow to get maximum results.

Includes:

- Participation in quarterly Master's Series of Workshops and Strategic Planning Sessions. ($14,200 Value)
- Full and unlimited access to the above for your team either via live webcast or in person. ($6,800 Value)
- Quarterly written plan of action. ($3,250 Value)

Layer Two: The Execution Layer—Getting Results Through Focused Action!
We'll work with you weekly and bi-weekly to make sure you are staying on track with the structured accountability and support to execute on your plan so you get the results you want.

Includes:

- Bi-weekly private, one-to-one coaching sessions. ($7,200 Value)
- Bi-weekly accountability checks-ins—takes just 5–10 min. each! ($1,250 Value)
- 24/7 Discussion forum support & weekly small group "hot seat" sessions to use as needed. ($2,400 Value)

Layer Three: The Business Development Layer—Consistent Progress Towards Level Three!
This is the detailed process we'll take you and your team through called the Level Three Road Map™ so that step-by-step we help you build out the systems, team, and internal controls you need to successfully reach Level Three.

Includes:

- Customized video training to coach your team in building your systems and controls. ($7,200 Value)
- Monthly small group Business Development Mastermind Sessions. ($2,500 Value)
- Full access to the complete Business Success Home Study Course Library. ($16,800 Value)

The Bottom Line—Guaranteed Results and a Proven Program!

We guarantee our clients results—IN WRITING—that within the first 12 months working together they'll enjoy a 200% ROI on their coaching fees or the program is free and they'll get a 100% no questions asked refund.

Plus, all our coaching clients are on a month-by-month agreement so we have to get them dramatic and reasonably quick results or we'd lose them as clients. Considering our average client is with us for several years it's clear they are getting real value.

The bottom is that you'll get the concrete action steps you need, along with the proven support and accountability structure, to take your business to the next level!

We'll start off each quarter with an in-person advanced business workshop and Strategic Planning Session to map out the coming quarter, then coach you weekly and bi-weekly to make sure you stay on track, execute on your plan, and get the results you want!

At the same time we'll make sure that each month you make real progress in building out the systems, team, and controls you need to build a business you can one day sell, scale, or even own passively.

Listen to What Our Clients Say...

Brian Fuchs
Windswept Marketing, Inc

"When I started with the coaching program less than a year ago I had a successful Middle Stage Level Two business that totally revolved around me. I was essentially a one man shop. The program has helped me to begin building my team and systems, both of which have reduced my business's dependence on me. **Currently, our team and systems handle 95% of our operations, freeing me up to begin to systematize our sales and marketing area of the business. The best part is that during this time we've literally *doubled* our profits!**"

Tiffany Prinster
DIYHCG.com

"The Maui program has helped me to grow intellectually and emotionally as a business woman. When I first joined the program at 23, I felt limited because I didn't have the business background and expertise to grow and expand it. The Maui team has helped me to build and utilize a team, incorporate systems, and develop simple business controls that have allowed me to step out of most of the everyday operations of my business and focus more on the 'big-picture' and growth of the company. Furthermore, the access to the advisor team has been invaluable. **One bit of coaching on a joint-venture partnership I was about to enter literally saved me $100,000 per year! You can't put a price tag on that.**"

Dana Smith
Exalt Resources

"The coaching program has helped me to develop the systematic processes to grow sales and improve the operations of my business. The road map the Maui team gave me has helped me spend more time on building my business (as opposed to doing the 'job' of my business) than ever before. **If you're someone who is thinking about joining the program then all I can say is don't let anything stop you—not the time, not the money, not anything. It's made a huge impact on our business.**"

Tom Santilli

xByte, Inc.
"I've reduced my working hours in half and still make the same 7-figure income. Only now don't come in to the office until after 10am and take every Friday off to be with my family for the weekend. This sure feels a lot more like wealth and freedom to me."

Marichel Ewert

Entrepreneur
"Through Maui I have learned to structure my appraisal company in such a way that **I have gone from working 40 hours a week to 2-3 hours a week and still make the same amount of money.**"

Brian Anderson

Hostek.com
"I used to be that person that worked 14-18 hour days (sometimes even more) 7 days per week. After going through your training I immediately started implementing the changes I learned. At that time I had a Level 2 business that totally revolved around me. Wow, what a difference the training made. I spent 10+ years working myself crazy and got to $1,000,000 in sales. After implementing the changes I learned, **our sales doubled in the last 4 years and I no longer have to work.** I now work (if you want to call it that) because I love what I do, not because I have to. Anyone that is serious about making a lifestyle change should dive in and learn all they can from David and the Maui team."

Kelly Fabros

The Mail Center
"The program has helped me build systems and controls, which used to scare me. **Plus in our first 6 months of the program we grew our sales by over 45%!**"

Dr. Gurpreet Padda
Surgeon and Entrepreneur

"I'm a surgeon with a thriving pain management and anti-aging practice. I'm also a serial entrepreneur with a dozen other businesses from restaurants, to medical billing services, to commercial real estate projects...the results speak for themselves—the program helped me to radically upgrade my use of time and make an **additional $1 million of net income.** I still use these same strategies and principles to this day and find them just as useful and profitable. **I don't see how any serious business owner can miss the opportunity to work with the Maui team and learn these and their other Level Three strategies."**

Dr. Kimberly Nguyen
Cottage Dental

"Over my last 12 months with the program my two dental offices have grown by 31% and 12% respectively. What's more, my stress level has gone down tremendously and my team really understands where we want to go, and how building the practice to Level Three is good for their own job stability . . . I would recommend the program to any business owner who wants to build a business, not a job. The program gives you a step-by-step, cookbook approach of exactly how to grow and develop your business as a business."

Ryan Arnold
Entrepreneur

"I built my last service business into an Advanced Stage Level Two business and **sold it for over $5 million. These ideas work, but you have to listen to the Maui team and put the ideas into action. It's totally up to you."**

Blake Schwank
Colorado Computer Support
"I've been part of the Business Coaching Program for 3 years now. In that time **we've quadrupled sales to over $1.8 million!**"

Mark Huha
Quality Property Maintenance, Inc.
"I been running our business for over a decade now and prior to learning about Maui Mastermind I was getting burned out. The business worked, but only if I was there every day for long hours to make it work. **In just our first year in the program our net income from the business is up by 44% and we finally broke $1 million in sales!** We have found the accountability that the Maui program holds us to is priceless in moving the process forward at a speed that we would NEVER do on our own. **If you are serious about building a successful business then my advice to you is to immediately get started working with the Maui team. It was one of the best business decisions I ever made."**